Rosamundo

poems by

Barbara de la Cuesta

Finishing Line Press
Georgetown, Kentucky

Rosamundo

ACKNOWLEDGMENTS

Thanks to The Massachusetts Cultural Council for a long ago fellowship that
started off this project.

Publisher: Leah Maines

Editor: Christen Kincaid

Cover Art: Woodcut by B. de la Cuesta

Author Photo: Paul Dresher

Cover Design: Elizabeth Maines McCleavy

Printed in the USA on acid-free paper.
Order online: www.finishinglinepress.com
           also available on amazon.com

Author inquiries and mail orders:
Finishing Line Press
P. O. Box 1626
Georgetown, Kentucky 40324
U. S. A.

Table of Contents

Waltham, Massachusetts

The governour and some companie with him went up by Charles River above Watertown and named the first brooke Beaverbrooke because beavers had shorn down divers dams across the north side of the river, being a fair streame and coming from a pond a mile below the river. Thence to a great rock upon which stood a high stone cleft in sunder that men might go through which they called Adams Chair.
        Governour Winthrop 1631

Priscilla Cycling to Work

Priscilla, cycling to work in milky dawn:
Saint Mary's rich red brick, hummocky lawn
already green from late March snow.
They're razing a fire-gutted house on Water Street.
She wonders what they'll put up in its place
and if they'll do it before summer.

Stops to buy a western egg at Alexander's
Waltham House of Pizza, eats it standing by her
bike, and watching welfare mothers climb
the stairs to number twenty-two, get at
their social workers early.

Tampon lying in the gutter. Unlovely
artifacts our age, she thinks.

The Charles River rushes below
Old Waltham Cotton and Wool Works,
It's elder housing now, and artists' studios,
Enoch Rowan, her great uncle, sold
the property to Francis Cabot Lowell,
another distant…who introduced
the power loom and built great mill on Elm Street.

Rowans moved to Watertown, did well
in snuff and mattress ticking, built large house
on Auburn Street. She remembers Christmas dinner
long ago, dressed up in velveteen.

A little late, but still she makes the little
detour at the Mill to take the little footbridge,
cross the river…

Her river, she calls it.
But it's not your river, Frostie remonstrates.

You always say that everything is yours.
It is, she says, insisting. I claim it. No one
 else does.
Well, if it were mine, I'd keep
it cleaner, he says.

Working on it, she. I have
a lot of people working on it...

Her committee, dragging rusty supermarket carts
and other unmentionable objects out of it.
But she was first, the first to claim it.

Frostie is relentless, his mother's son.
He brings up Mount Feake Cemetery where they picnicked,
ducks at Roberts, The Red Line and the Blue...
You always talk as if you owned them.

Well I do! She carries the joke to ever
grander heights hyperbole. Back in
those heady years she asked for the divorce—
and freed the three of them from eight room house,
two Volvos, lawn, two dogs—they owned the Red Line.

 And the Blue...
Futuristic bullet streaking through
its tiled corridor to
        WONDERLAND

They never took it there, but to AQUARIUM,
and up the creaky escalator to the Bay State Liners:
Edward Rowe Snow, gently rocking, waiting,
hers. She claimed it too, also the harbor
and one island, hers.

You ought to keep it cleaner, Frostie says.
Well, she's been working on it, such responsibility.

It was necessary to divest some pieces of it
here and there: the Red Line, all the islands
but for Peddocks—

You could camp there free, and it had a ghost town,
nature walks at ten and one, all free.
And, coming back from Peddocks filthy, they would make
for her restroom at the Marriott, wash up
in marble splendor.

She kept the washroom. But she couldn't be bothered
keeping all of it, she told Frostie.

Her empire.
Frostie understood, for all the joking.
Solie didn't. She thought Priscilla's empire
wasn't worth the losses.

But these other people, Ma, that use
our island and our washroom. Do you give permission?
Sure, I tell them, go ahead, it's free.
You have to be, too, free, she tells him.

Free to see it's yours, she lectures, but
he squirms. He likes her flights.
But how, Ma? Do you give them tickets?
No, of course not. I have administrators,
like the MDC.

And that's yours too?
Of course.

The river rushes under her, reduced and concentrated, below the dam.
It makes her lightheaded. She leaves the leafy bower and crosses the
parking lot to Moody. The water over the dam is loud in the early
morning calm. A nephew of Elihu Rowan, son of Enoch, Seth, incurred
a gentlemanly debt at Harvard College, and sold the head of the water

on the Charles to the Lowells for the equivalent of a mess of lentils. He sold the power source!
Oh, her family ran to idiots and scoundrels!

Passing Grover Cronin's, Crescent Street, The Irish Travel Bureau.

The great house on Mount Auburn Street was let in rooms in 1900, to girls that worked in the Mill. It houses, now, retarded citizens. Let it go. Priscilla wouldn't want a son of hers inheriting the fruit of others' labor, incurring gentlemanly debts at Harvard College.

She has to give a pint of blood before work, for Terry in the office who suffers with familial polycystic disease, and had a hemorrhage on Friday.

A hundred and seventy miles above the Earth, Columbia passes over gypsum sands, the Tularosa Basin. Young and Crippen sleep. Some of the almost forty thousand tiles on the spaceship are missing, but it shouldn't present a problem say the experts.

She follows the yellow dots on the ground floor of the Nichol's wing, misses turn and has to ask…It's three doors back and down the ramp. She stretches on black vinyl, closes her eyes and thinks of Terry…Ever had malaria? she's asked. Not she knows of…Terry's kidneys form cysts that burst and bleed. He has a brother suffers from the same, and also a small son. She feels the tourniquet, the pinch, and overpowering tiredness even though the day's only beginning. You want some coffee? No, she has to go

Besides Columbia, 1,156 other crafts of one description or another are in orbit, as are 3,419 pieces of debris: spent rocket bodies, nuts and bolts…

She coasts on Frostie's Nishiki the final half a mile
to her first patient…well, you call them consumers now.
East windows of the hospital are glinting in pale sunlight.
Highland Street to Prospect, Vincent's Florists
are setting out narcissus bulbs. Van Houten is
a rather run down street,

But someone's painting a cottage pink, gray trim.
A duplex is being sheathed in yellow vinyl,
all of Waltham being sheathed, it seems, M. Girardeau and Son.
She thinks she couldn't live in vinyl, under vinyl.

Robert Frost wanted to live under thatch…
but she prefers solidity of yellow brick. The projects
being yellow brick, will make good ruins.
She couldn't live in a building that wouldn't molder well.

A house is almost immortal when you compare it
to a body, Rika, her mother, says.
Years now, she's been constructing the house in Ipswich
as a new enclosure for her soul,

And all the time not letting Harry touch
her body. Harry pays for most of it:
the bath done over in a celery shade of tile,
the cherry cabinets, and now the solarium…

Not for Priscilla. It costs too much.

Not she doesn't see the fires that burn
within the project, leave their scorch around
the windows and the doors. A solid ruin,
but she'd have been more generous had she built it—
dream builder that she was, like Rika.

Still, she's lucky to have her unit in
the elder's section. She likes to live above
their wheelchairs and benches where they sun themselves
like turtles. Four flights up and insulated from
the teeming families of Buildings A and B.

She locks her bike to a swingless swing set outside 440.
The sisters' house, inherited from their builder father.
Also yellow brick, but older, and redolent

of Catholic rectories, especially in this hallway
with its umbrella stand and cloudy mirrors.

Enedina, the night girl gives report: Adie and Winnie, as usual, slept
through the night. Megan, as usual, didn't. Had to pee on hour mostly, read
her magazines, and bent Enedina's ear with information on astronomy,
history, politics. Enedina doesn't mind this—unlike some others, treats her
nicely, and the other two lovingly, like her babies, changing their diapers
gently. Enedina comes from Guatemala. You write and I'll get them up,
Priscilla tells her.
No, I write all wrong.
Just copy mine from yesterday. It's all the same.
You need to learn, she tells her, so Enedina writes and she goes up.

Winnie Blakey wakes, says, Innerspring.
Admiral Farragut, she says after a pause.
Her sister Megan's radio, set to WCRB, comes on
in the middle of a Scarlatti sonata, whirling, climbing…
Mandible, says Winnie. Megan wakes, sits halfway up,
and picks up a copy of Opera News from the file at the foot of her bed.

Am I alive? asks Adie, the other sister.
Priscilla gravely takes her pulse. Yes, seems you are, Priscilla says,
aware that moment of her own aliveness, lightened by
her crossings and recrossings of the river, by bloodletting,
and Scarlatti on Megan's clock radio,

Something pulling down, however…Solie. Was it a hickey
that she noted on Solie's neck last night? There's been
a Puerto Rican boy hanging about. Male child turned to menace.
You take us to live among Puerto Ricans, see what you get, say Solie's eyes.
Their new life, to Soli, wasn't worth the losses.
Well it's done and can't be un…

She goes to Megan. Cesare Siepi of Milan played Figaro in 1948, Megan
reads out of her magazine. Whirling, climbing… Hello, my dear. I'll have
the bedpan and lie up a little while. She brings it, and goes back to lay out

the sisters' housedresses, then hot water for Winnie's oatmeal. Checks back on Megan. It's still coming, Megan says. It stops and starts. I can't sleep peacefully a couple hours even.

It's the diuretic. Why don't you go ahead and wet the bed like Adie. I can change it… Priscilla says, and in an instant she could bite her tongue out of her head.

It's a grudge I have against the Universe that it's so poorly arranged that this old body can't get to the toilet so you must spend your day bringing bedpans and can't be with your children…
They don't need me. They're in school
I'd chloroform all three of us if I could walk around.
Oh, stop it!
If you had any sense you'd help me.
Help you what?
You know very well. You have control of all our pills. Those little blue ones would do it.
They count you know. When the nurse comes, she counts.
Well, I'm thinking people do miscount. Things fall on floors, roll under registers…
I simply don't fancy dying the way we all know I will.
How's that?
Well drowning, in my fluids.
I've heard that drowning's not so bad. Peaceful rather.
Who said that?
Oh, something I heard, or read…
You should be more accurate. You have no scientific curiosity. When the Bookmobile comes I'll request a proper book.

A good idea. She's having night thoughts, Priscilla thinks. The daytime Megan thinks exclusively of murdering her sisters, not herself.

Not going to school today, says Adie, under the covers. Oh, yes you are.

Priscilla fishes in the drawer for underwear. There're fifteen single stockings in there, not one pair. The half have seams. She wonders do they sell them that way still, or has Adie kept them since the forties?

Jaysus, Mother Mary! Adie cries. Why don't I die?
And Enedina, just then leaving, says, Hush you.
What would God think? He can hear you.

Megan, listening, appalled, the ignorance. She disbelieves in god herself, but thinks that he'd approve of Adie's sentiment in case he did exist. She'd chloroform them both, of course, if she could get away with it. She studies a photo in *Opera News* of Mildred Meller of Cleveland, Ohio playing Cherubino. A nice role. Another of Alicia della Casa, of Burgdorf Switzerland in the same part. She had a smaller success. The Swiss are a phlegmatic race. Don't often produce an artist of first rank. She dozes a minute, wakes to find Priscilla there.

Do you know, Priscilla asks, if they still make stockings that have seams?

Oh, dear me, yes. Megan sits up and eases into her yellow housecoat. I'll get up, she says. And laboriously getting down from the high bed which had been her parents' she handholds her way from one piece of furniture to another, into the little bathroom and makes a cup of tea with hot water from the tap. The tremors are not too bad this morning, and she manages to get the yellow pill that Priscilla places in her hand down her long and sensitive throat.

You'll get *The Globe* so I can start the crossword.
Soon's I have a minute, Priscilla says, making up the bed.

Nine-thirty, and Columbia is over western Australia, belly up so the cargo bay when opened is not exposed to sunlight…

Oh Jaysus, Mother Mary, take me! Adie
crows, and Winnie wakes to contemplate

a cyclist on her ceiling. He has a number
seventy-seven on his chest
she puzzles over.

And the sheet that under Adie was warm
and moist
has now grown cold
and clammy.

A kind of hybrid, this Columbia. Climbed to orbit as a rocket, it cruises now like a spaceship, and tomorrow it will glide to landing like a powerless aircraft.

Once she gets the pill down, Megan feels a little better. Yes, she tells Priscilla, there was a comic on the radio who used to say she was so poor she couldn't afford stockings, so she painted a black line up the back of each leg. She stops in her return from bathroom to take the cover off Billy's cage and whistles to him Cleopatra's aria from act two of Handel's *Julius Caesar.* Billy fluffs his feathers, tries a note. She makes her way back to the bed and sits on it, gets her panties on, but cannot manage bra. Enedina comes in with her coat on and *The Globe.*

Lovey Mother…
Adie raised five kids alone, and now her energy, trapped in a geriatric chair, has gone to nattering. If she could die…her daughters think, and call God's wisdom into question for the first time in their lives. *Pleasantly confused*, is

Dr. Tanzer's diagnosis.

Megan doesn't see what's pleasant. Wearing everybody's nerves, her own included, and doesn't even *know* us!

Mandible, says Winnie. A cascade of complex trills from Billy.

Winnie, up in her chair now too, notes old woman
with the hat on across the street, the one
that sells the waffles and the hot cakes, she tells Priscilla.

What?

The woman sells the hotcakes, wears a pillbox
hat. We sisters used to wear them year
we started bringing fellows home
to meet our Pa.

They had cerebral accidents, all three sisters, only Megan kept her wits.
Fight, she used to tell them. Fight like I do, but they wouldn't, allowed
themselves to slip into their present selves.

*An article on the front page of The Boston Globe calls the shuttle flight a shot
in the arm for the nation's spirit…following an time of sapping of the public
confidence.*
*"But now, Columbia restores us to a sense we're not the paralyzed giant of our
darkest self image."*

Priscilla hurries back to Megan's room.

Harry Truman could quote lines from "Locksley Hall".
That's Tennyson if you'll remember,
says Megan. Priscilla can't get taken up with this.
She's got Adie on the commode and Clifford across the hall.
"S" in Harry S, know what it stands for?
Nothing. In Ulysses S. it's Simpson…
Clifford's bath, then Wolfie, and a quick stop
at Jesús Roldán, and Alcide Arsenault…
Eulalie's…

   "To err is Truman," people used to say, says Megan.
   Still there was music in him, Harry.
   Grant, they used to say--Ulysses S—
   he couldn't even whistle Yankee Doodle.
   There was music in him,
   Harry, yes…

"The man that hath not music in himself,
nor is not moved by concord of sweet sound…
is fit for treason, strategems and spoils;

his soul is dark as Erebus. Let no
such man be trusted…"

Megan quotes
    Shakespeare, case you didn't…

Yes, this present inhabitant of the White House,
one suspects he has no music in him,
though he has a son must dance…

I told them fight, says Megan. They wouldn't. Now listen to them. We'll stick around, we used to tell each other, see how things turn out…like if they prove or disprove the Big Bang, you know, theory.

April 13, 1981, Columbia's in its second day. A couple cancellations makes its launch date same as Yuri Gargarin's historic flight in Vostok.

Step, step, slowly, Clifford comes along the hall, his clean clothes clutched in a little pile. Step, step, stopping by the kitchen clock. It's half past nine, and Priscilla's running late. Oh, Jaysus, Mother Mary, help me! Adie, left on the commode with Posey belt. Her sister Megan has turned to the crossword puzzle in *The Globe*. A harpsicord from the Hubbard Works is eased into a city van for transportation to the Public Library. Mr. Franklin Honey, Sexton of the Congregational Church affixes the sermon topic to the notice board…
    THE BROTHER OF THE…
Step, step, Clifford stops at the hallway mirror, sticks out his tongue and studies it, while Priscilla sits on the radiator, resting her feet. I had a good B.M., he tells her, in case you want to note it down…
    THE BROTHER OF THE PRODIGAL

A native of Gdansk, five letters. Megan is temporarily stumped.

COLD, cries Adie.

This day in l955, the Salk vaccine announced to public. A complex low is covering the Northeast. High pressure is building in the Midwest, will reach New England late tomorrow.

Gird for war. Six down.

Clifford arrives at bathroom, sits, takes off a shoe, a sock. He slowly places sock in shoe, in spite it's going in the wash. Another shoe, a sock. She hopes Adie will be O.K. She runs the water. Now the shirt. She helps him with the buttons. Turns off the water. Three buttons, four. It's off, and he insists on folding it. He was an engineer. Worked on the Hoover Dam. Now trousers. The water's getting cold. Now underpants. He has to go, picks up his pale old shriveled member, pees a feeble stream, shakes off a drop, another. There.

Four hundred people trying to reach news of the astronauts forget to put 500 before the official number, get, instead, a Claremont, California housewife.

Spilled his seed, sixteen across. That's Onan, in that Dirty Old Book. Dolomite...

An Alp, that is, thinks Megan.

It's ten-fifteen, and Clifford's bath proceeds at
stately pace. Step, step, slowly, reaching
for the handhold. Priscilla helps. He's in.
The water's tepid. He takes the soap and traces
circles on his chest, his belly.
She pours shampoo and washes his pink old spotty
head and rinses.

I wasn't finished, he says. It can't be helped. The water's cold, not good for you. She towels him, leaves him dressing, seated in the bath chair, rushes back to Adie.

Cold! says Adie. Leave me to my death with drafts around my hips!

Priscilla walks her—listing like some old car that's had its chassis knocked askew—back to the geriatric chair and wheels her out to waiting van that takes her to the Sunshine Club.

Scholar President, reads Megan. Jefferson. He fancied Homer. Must be Jefferson, but doesn't fit with L from seven down, unless…Ah, yes, it's peccary a kind of pig…. You're back, my dear, I'm reading here they vote today, this issue of school prayer…

At the Sunshine Club

At the Sunshine Club, Rebecca, the director, passes jelly donuts. Adie asks her, Are you my mother, Lovey? No, I'm not your mother, Adie. I'm Rebecca, and I'm thirty-three years old, and you're a hundred, she instructs. Her birthday today, Adie. They've planned a celebration.

I am? cries Adie. Gracious!

Mayor Clark's invited, and the *News Tribune.*

So, I couldn't be your mother, could I? says Rebecca.
Reality Orientation is the term. Rebecca sometimes thinks; she doesn't blame them caring for it not a jot—reality.

Yes, *you're* a mother, Adie. You've a daughter and three sons that live in Somerville, another
daughter somewhere and seventeen grandchildren.

Do I? I never heard of any such a thing.

Alcide Arsenault
At 508, next door, escapes his wife,
and with his Walk-Aid makes his way downtown
by way of Crescent Street, and past the Irish Travel Bureau,
seeing ghosts:

The old Hall's Corner Smoke Shop,
Lovings' Furnishings for Men,
Ike Allen's Corinthian Alleys in the basement
under the Waldorf Lunch on Gordon Street,
and the old Embassy—
a walkway now.

It had a ceiling that gave an illusion of a starry night...

Meanwhile Eulalie opens the front door to Priscilla. He's gone, Eulalie says, I hid his walk aid but he found it.

No, not again, the second time this week. She mounts her bike and heads down Main Street.

But Alcide is on Moody Street in little park where the Embassy Theater used to be.

A starry sky,

Alcide recalls, with floating clouds. A rather taking thing.
J. Lesley Cahill played the organ.

...READING FROM EURIPIDES
    THE LECTURE ROOM AT
        SPINGOLD...runs round the electric sign on the Waltham
Savings.

The wonders of the modern world, thinks Alcide.
But give him any day the starry sky at the
old Embassy, billiards at Ike Allen's,
trolley trips to Norumbega, French-American
Athletic and Literary Association, met
on the second floor of the Odd Fellows..

Alcide is watching the river scum wash up in little inlet under the Gold
Star Mother's Bridge when Priscilla spots him from a rise two blocks away.

There used to be a dance hall on those pilings,
he's thinking. Nuttings. The Black Velvet Irish Band,
Prince Edward Isle Quadrille...

He suddenly decides to have a beer in O'Reilly's Daughter, hails a passing
cab.

A toasted dungbeetle, reads Megan, has a crisp exterior and, inside, a
texture like souffle (the answer to last week's acrostic)

At the Sunshine Club little Jerome Aucoin, who's come by with his mother
to visit Great Aunt Adie on her birthday, wears a polo shirt from Disney
World. He's three years old; holds up three fingers when he's asked. Adults
get quite excited when he does this. But he's run away because they want
to know the name he's chosen for his baby sister when she comes out of
his mother's tummy. Now he hides behind a table, spilling tiny pieces of a
puzzle. Auntie, in a funny chair says
    Lovey Mother.
    And he sees—her knees are spread—she wears a diaper like his own,

and that she's wet it

The usual? Melissa asks, and pushes a Michelob in front of Alcide. Fresh still, he notes. She's only forty-seven, she's told him. Has she got her teeth still, he wonders? A little overweight, of course, but he prefers that in a woman. He likes to see it high on hips the way Melissa….Saucy. He would bet she's got her teeth…

I'm just wondering, Alcide dares, you got your own…?

My what?

Teeth. Your own teeth. Alcide grins and shows his full upper and lower.

Well, six of them. Four up, two down, Melissa grins back. Just thought you'd check me out, eh, Alcide?

That's a lovely picture, Bobby, says Rebecca at the Sunshine Club to Bobby Rosier who is simple. And you colored in the lines.

It's going to be snow flowers tomorrow, Berta Bechtel says. I heard it on the weather.

Rosa from the Agency

Rosa, from the agency, waits for the Auburndale bus at the corner of Flint and Adams. She had to leave Laureano up on the ladder inspecting the chimney flashing. Now she'll have to worry about him the whole day. Seventy-five years old and walking around on roofs. Always, it is something. Yesterday it was the officer coming about the cocks in the yard. "You have to catch them and put them in a cage today," she told him at breakfast. He thinks he can carry on however he wants, being Puerto Rican and legal. He forgets her own vulnerability to cops snooping around. And all the Guatemalans in the rented basement. They attract attention too. Does he ever think of that?

At least she goes in comfort on a bus. She used to have to walk to her jobs when they lived out in the suburbs in the other house that he had built with his own hands. Oh, he was strong then. Only trouble was he built it without getting any permits, so, even after they wasted large sums on lawyers, the town tore it all down. Just let things be quiet for a while, she tells the Virgin. Let me go to my work in peace.

Out the window she sees the couple in jogging shorts who walk along Mount Feake Avenue. He's always in front and stands waiting for her at corners with a stopwatch in his hand. She's a little woman with sturdy legs, and walking behind her taller husband reminds Rosa of her own people scouring the sierra for firewood, the woman always behind with a pile of sticks on her head. The man stalking ahead. They have their pride, men. Ask them to come down off a ladder so you can go to work in peace and they have to say no.

She gets off at Fletcher. Sees Priscilla from the agency on her bicycle. Alcide has run away from Eulalie again.

I thought she hide his walker.

He found it. You look on Crescent Street. I'll ride up Moody.

She shouldn't hide his walker. He has his pride like all of them. She looks into the Irish Travel Bureau. Sometimes he goes in there. Most likely he's at the used car lot. They keep offering him a job there, and he doesn't know it's a joke. Well, let Priscilla look there. She has the bicycle. Other days, he sits in the little park where he told her the Embassy Theater used to be.

It had a sky full of stars painted on the ceiling, he told her.

And an organ There was never anything like it.

But Alcide's not in the park either. She can see around the corner of the bank that it's empty. She abandons this—can't waste anymore time, with Wolfie waiting—crosses Moody again and takes the little path beside the sluice gates to The Mill and up the elevator to Wolfie, waiting in his motorized wheelchair for his bath.

Come, me, he says, his words little explosions that you stand around waiting for him to finish, wanting to help him, but how? She stands over him and he puts his arms around her hips and buries his head in her belly. Soft, soft, he murmurs, the words coming easier. She lets him, just because the words come easier.

Her belly cramps So as to keep up her self respect a little, Rosa needs to recall how Wolfie's caresses began, how apologetic he had been, and worshipful, not of Rosa but of some idea he had of woman.

Ooman.

He got the word out one day as she bent to help him into his chair. He had his good hand on her waist, so he could feel where her hip swelled out.

Rosa like her mother, was *una mujer bien plantada*.

Woman. He ran his fingers over her hip thinking some other words he couldn't say. He was almost like the midwife in Zoyatla, *misia* Fernanda, sizing up Mondo's approaching birth, was she wide enough?

All this was outside her clothes. Like a blind man figuring the shape of a once familiar object. Another time she needed to bend over him to brush his hair, he weighed her right breast with his good hand and moaned. Then his eyes asked forgiveness, poor man; he suffered more than she did during this stage of his studying her. She couldn't help it, her right breast was wishing away the cloth of her blouse, her bra.

Shameless woman.

Sometimes, like a doctor or a priest, his eyes questioned her, as if he wanted her to explain to him what all this meant. Then her own thoughts hid themselves. How could she say what her breast desired?

And all this time, and even before, she saw him helpless and naked in the

bath chair. As he stood holding her shoulders, she washed his thighs and
buttocks and behind his scrotum, only handing him the washcloth, as she'd
been instructed in the classes, for him to wash his own penis.

His body was beautiful to Rosa, his skin
white and spotless like her aunt's gardenia
blossoms. His affected legs gone back to a
child's smooth unmuscled body.

In the chapel of the Italian Church
there was a nearly naked figure
of Jesus laid across his mother's lap,
reminded Rosa of Wolfie.

Wolfie was a Jew like Jesus, Rosa
knew, but didn't believe what some said about
it was the Jews killed Jesus. Why would they kill
their own, their beautiful son?
There had to be some other explanation.

Wolfie was painfully thin. Under the arch
of his ribs his stomach was hollow,
like the cavern beneath the ribs of
the crucified Jesus. To Rosa this
was achingly sad.

She was a student of crucifixes and had
her own large plaster figure in her bedroom.
She'd bought it at a yard sale and felt rich
in religious art since hanging it over the bed.
Laureano called it the *estatua de la mala muerte*
and accused it of coming into his dreams.

To Rosa the great arch under the breastbone
represented suffering: the strain of the
raised arms supporting the weight of the body.
She wondered if the little peg securing the feet

offered any relief. But probably it hurt
too much to rest weight on it.

Usually the face, fallen over like a wilted flower,
reflected patience or resignation;
the pain was there in the great arch of ribs
and the hollow beneath.

Wolfie didn't eat enough to keep himself nourished and sometimes had
to have a feeding tube. Rosa could coax him and make sure he ate. Before
she went to him regular, sometimes she would look over at his table at the
Sunshine Club and note that the aides had put the tray beyond his reach or
had not removed all the little lids on the bowls and cups.

She was guilty of taking more time about Wolfie's bath, for example, than
she did with a man like Clifford. She had also studied him seriously,
taking time to straighten his bad arm and flex the fingers, making sure to
thoroughly wash inside the clenched palm.

You couldn't see the penis of the figure in
the Italian Church; she thought it must
be well developed like Wolfie's. It was the largest
penis she had ever seen. And the only Jewish one.

She wasn't sure what this meant.
Usually it nestled fatly in
its nest of curly hair between his legs.
A sleeping animal.

But sometimes, like her breast, it woke
and had something it wanted; then they both
looked at it with concern.

For a long time, in any case, Rosa knew his flesh, while her flesh could only
wish the clothes away. If he wanted to know hers, he must advance on his
own. She knew if he did she would not scream or put in a complaint as
some of the aides had done. That was all she knew.

Then, when summer came, one day she wore a loose little chemise with slender shoulder straps and the bra built in, so that you didn't have two sets of straps. It was pretty and not the sort of thing she usually wore unless it was very hot out. He couldn't take his eyes off of it while she helped him undress for his bath; and once she got him seated on the bath chair the sleeping penis came out of its nest and stood up proudly. Rosa laughed and they were comfortable enough together by then that he laughed too, and then into the loose chemise went his hand and found her bare nipple. She couldn't help gasping in pleasure.

Oomen, he groaned. Ooman!

And then he found the flesh at her middle and her hip and her belly, and then he knew, dear man, that her breast was calling him back to the nipple; and that was enough to bring Rosa, so long she had been waiting.

So Rosa came to represent Woman to Wolfie, and he worshipped her; and she accepted his worship.

But it was a sin, Rosa told herself. And now they were both punished.

Rosa had taken up the study of sin when she used to teach the catechism classes to the little Mexican children at St. Barnabas. There were little sins and big sins and if you committed too many little sins you were more likely to go on to the big ones. Some sins you did in your mind and then, sometimes, you went on to let yourself fall into them. This was the kind of sin she and Wolfie were doing. But Rosa never felt this quite covered the study of sin, and had her own thoughts about it.

Rosa got her monthly in the night, three weeks late, heavy with clots like the one passes now with a clutching of her womb.

Now. Bath, she says,
Bath, it's late, her words coming easy also, because she talks to him like a baby, not needing to put together the unfamiliar sentences she learned in night school.

He puts a hand under her blouse and fondles her left breast, she takes off his pajama top and unties and slips down the bottoms. His sex is purple and hard. It has no failures like his legs or his speech. She pushes him into the bathroom. Lock door, he tries to say, and she does this carefully as usual. He's able to swing himself into the bath chair, while she slips the bottoms down and off. She starts the water until it's the right warmth, then throws the lever to start the shower.

He was a lawyer, Wolfie. A good lawyer. Or a lawyer who was good. Helped people like herself get legal: Inez Flores, and Mercedes Lozano, legal for twenty years. She, herself, came along after his stroke, but she knows he'd help her if he could.

If Laureano would marry her, she'd be legal too, but no use thinking about that. She sits on the tub edge to soap him, her hair filling with droplets of spray. His hand goes up her skirt and finds the bloody pad. It doesn't shame her. Wolfie never shames her, he's so curious and serious in his examinations of her, like a doctor.

Alcide always asks women if they still bleed. If they still bleed and have their teeth. He's crazy to know and asks before he even knows your name. She's over fifty, and only has about half her teeth, but she still bleeds enough for two women, Rosa thinks as she feels another rush of warm blood.

He has his hand now, right up inside her panties, and another on her nipple. She is going to come, she thinks. It's disgraceful he can do this to her, when all of Laureano's pumping above her merely makes her tired. Touch, touch! Wolfie cries, and she cradles his penis as she comes, comes comes…oh, oh, oh, her womb is leaping inside her.

She should be ashamed. How can she not be ashamed? But it gives him such pleasure. And her too, she admits. On his face is a look, as if it was him who just came, came, came… How can it make him so happy when he can't come in her properly. When Enedina got legal, she told Rosa, Wolfie was as happy as she was. Dear man, she says, and puts her lips to his.

Then she's all business. It's Ten-thirty. Wolfie needs to go down to the

Sunshine Club for juice and cookies and Reality Orientation where they tell you what day it is and when the next holiday is coming, things he knows perfectly well and the others are just as happy not knowing. What is so important about reality when you're fastened in a geriatric chair, Rosa wonders.

As usual, he wants his shirt and tie, as if he's going to business,poor man. He looks happy this morning, as if he's brought off the most wonderful thing in making her come on the ledge of the bathtub at ten in the morning. She wants to kiss him again, but abstains.

Sometimes she dreams about what it would have been like if she'd known him when he was all himself. Of cours she knows that he had a wife then and a big practice. Kids who live in California now. But still she likes to think of him caring for her then, a woman on the side, of course. She would have been younger, maybe she would have given him a baby, even though she hadn't been able to give one to Laureano. It would have been a smart kid and studious and careful, unlike Mondo who is presently in jail for painting on an underpass. And white. Wolfie is very white, almost blue in his whiteness. And black, black hair. Both of our hairs are straight and black. But Wolfie is a Jew, and Jews have their ways, maybe different than most men. They were like Turkos, like the Syrians in the drygoods stores at homes.

She combs his hair nicely and takes him down to the Sunshine Club for cookies.

Priscilla gives up Alcide, returns to Megan.
Tycho, saw a supernova as a boy. Eleven down, says Megan. That's Brahe. He was a great astronomer. He had his nose cut off in a duel and wore a false one made of silver, or gold, I can't remember…Priscilla's supposed to get her and Winnie to the birthday party in the van at one o'clock. Won't be easy. She's prepared to fail.

The Mayor, says Megan. What do I want to see the Mayor for? I know all about He has fourteen children and brags about it. I didn't vote for him. I never vote for Catholic or Irish.
How do you know which are, which aren't? Priscilla asks.

I read the literature they send you, every word. Those that aren't Catholic don't go bragging about ten children and graduate from B.C. and Holy Cross where they learn football and some Latin. Fourteen children. You'd think that some of them might have heard of such a thing as *interruptus—coitus interruptus*… In spite of it's being Latin, it's not a thing they'll teach you at B.C. One, I had. A single brat. You ask me how? *Coitus Interruptus*, that's how. Priest ridden race.

I saved myself. It wasn't easy. Get you when you're weak and helpless.

Alcide Still at Large

The boys from the Press Box are lounging in the settling body of an old Pontiac in the lot of Masserelli Motors. Batty Allard, Berto Ginastero, Cristos Demos, Jacko Winegar:

Hey, Alcide, lookin' for a job again?

Don't Jacko. Don't you see that he believes you?

Naa, he don't. Nice job out front, with coat and tie; you meet the public…

Listen Frenchy, it's just a joke, says Cristos.

A joke?

Yes, he's just kidding you.

A coat, he said, a tie. I'd meet the public.

A joke. He's only joking, Alcide baby. We ain't got no public here. You tell me, you see any public? Cristos waves his arms around the muddy lot. And what you want to work for, anyhow? You got yourself nice pension from Canadian…

U.S. Army. Alcide straightens up his shoulders. U.S. Army.

Well, you shouldn't go believing every little…

Meet the public…Alcide murmurs as he turns the corner at the French American Victory Society. He took Eulalie here to dances in his uniform, the Sixteenth Infantry. It was the year they opened up the second front. He can still remember Tranquille Galant behind the drums in his Navy whites, and Claude, Eulalie's brother, fiddling. He had one leg shorter than the other, so he didn't go off to war when the rest of them…

A largish crested bird is strutting just
ahead of Alcide on the sidewalk. He turns
his pocket out, shakes out the crumbs. The U. S. Army,
he served in. The Navy was what he wanted, but
they wouldn't take him because of his missing finger,
so it was the Army, late in the conflict.

Embarrassing, it was to be around
in civvies so long, and going to the kitchen
rackets in Irish Town every night.
They used to call it The Bleachery. A crazy time.
The French, Italians, Irish whirled together
by the war. They married, many of them—
French to Irish, Irish to Italian.

Tranquille and Jean Pierre were bedded down
with Irish girls before they'd finished training.
And he was having his first woman. Irish Peg,
they called her; used to charge a dollar to
the uniforms, had little ratlike teeth
that nibbled at him... U.S. Army. Zut!
He scatters a crowd of grackles, sparrows; crosses
the tracks below the car wash. Used to be
a school here, the Misses Varnums: made Americans
out of you. Combated Bolshevism
and Lawlessness in the Foreign Born...

Priscilla's back from the Bookmobile. They have nothing on the Nile or the
Tudor Queens.
    They specialize, it seems, in romantic fiction and popular biography.
She's found a book on Queen Elizabeth.
    Elizabeth the Which? asks Megan.
    The Second.
    Ach! The world's most boring woman. Take it back. The world's most
boring woman! All she ever thinks about are dogs and horses.

Yes Alcide sees it now, his memory a lucid pool,
The creamy walls, projected stereoptican ghosts,
Lewis and Clark on shores of the Mississippi.
The terrible Miss Varnum, who would make Eulalie
leave the Monday wash to write her essay:
Why I Want to be a Citizen...

She took them berry picking, wouldn't let
the girls mix with the dirty boys.
She thought she'd hold that tide back,
till the War undid her.

Yes, married, most of them, a half breed
in the oven, by the Second Front.
Jean Pierre, Tranquille, and he, soon after,
to the prim Eulalie. She got word

of Irish Peggy. He never had her after that.
He sees her still sometimes.

She turned to drink, got skinnier than ever.
Never had enough to eat until that Jew
that owned The Buckle kept her, fattened her up.
He saw her last in a respectable gray suit that
strained against her spreading bottom, going to those
meetings they had now, in the basements
of the churches.

He stops to watch two boys who've caught a fish—a bass—from off the bridge at Moody Street. It's huge almost a foot and a half in length. They'll never get it up; the line's too light and they haven't got a net with a handle long enough to reach it.

That tea, you know, that ended up in Boston Harbor, Megan tells Priscilla, was traded to the Indians for opium and sold to the British. The Indians from India, that is, not Redskins. The mayor's phoned to say he's running late, will be there in less than fifteen minutes. Albert, getting bored with waiting, opens his pants and begins to slide them... Lookit! Alva Otting shrieks. Rebecca goes: You mustn't, Albert. Cannot do that here. She pulls them up and fastens them. You want a cigarette? She walks him to a table. Dirty! Alva scolds.

The bass they've caught off Moody Street expires slowly at the end of the line. There's nothing to be done, till finally a passerby with a penknife cuts it. The biggest fish that's probably ever been seen in the Charles River, says the owner of the knife. Just too bad they didn't bring a net with a long handle. The coin collectors at the White Cloud Laundromat on Prospect Street are being forced with a pair of pliers. Two white kids, one black. They get away with twenty dollars and sixty cents.

Alcide pushes the traffic button, brings the north and south-bound traffic on Prospect Street to a halt.

A listener to WHYY calls to ask if Young and Crippen can make out the Great Wall of China. No, says a former astronaut who's manning phones. It's things like highways and ship's wakes you can see. The factor's contrast. You can see the Houston Astrodome, but not who's winning. Young and Crippen wake and are instructed to look down on the Kennedy Space Center below. Man, that is so pretty, is Crippen's comment. They check the cargo bay and open the clamshell doors to check for warps. The spaceship undergoes tremendous stresses, moving from night to day at intervals of ninety minutes.

The kid they call The Maggot wakes on the landing of the second story of Building D—the wags have named it Maggot's Landing—makes his way to the railroad trestle where The Professor waits with a bottle of Lambrusco and a discourse on the relation of the space-time continuum to Cream of Wheat. Priscilla asks if Megan wants a novel…Novels? No, I haven't any truck with novels! Megan says. I'm eighty-six years old; I haven't time for fiction. Fact! Yes, fact is stranger than…Rasputin, take Rasputin. Strange. They couldn't kill him, did you know…? They gave him poison, shot him six or seven times and still he's on his legs. That Alexandra, she's the one that caused the Russian revolution. She couldn't keep her finger out. He was her pet, Rasputin.

Coat and tie, thinks Alcide.
And meet the public. He crosses at the corner of Hammond Street,
and to calm himself he sits on a bench
and feeds the pigeons pretzels from his pockets.
Pigeons strut on their red legs.
If there weren't so many of them, Alcide thinks,
you might say they were beautiful…

Calm now, and, feeling both hunger and an urge, he thinks he'll have the eggplant parmigiana, use the bathroom at Mama Josie's. A block away and suddenly the urge is…

Merde! A woman with her little daughter by the hand is shrieking on the corner of Prospect and Newton.

Merde! Alcide fastens up his trousers. He's done it neatly as any dog, there in the gutter, but now the woman's screaming. Officer, this child has had to witness this filthy act! Her cry is taken up by the crowd that gathers, brings Lieutenants Langille and Mackle on their break in Dunkin Donuts.

Yes, Ma'm, we'll take him in. They pull him into the parking lot. We've told you, Mr. Arsenault. Here, get in the cruiser. This time we'll have to take you in.

Merde, merde!

But instead they take him to Eulalie: Going to have to watch him, Missus.

Watch him! You try!

A woman's little girl…

I turn my back a second!

Second time. A woman's little girl…what can we do? We ought to take him to the station, book him on indecency… Officer Langille is blushing, softening, pushing him toward her. He's a second cousin once removed.

Luncheon at the Sunshine Club

At the Sunshine Club they're making meatloaf, lemon jello. When I was in the hospital with my stroke, this little priest, his wafers in a leather case, surprises me, Megan tells Priscilla. Don't you come in here, I told him. I've no dealings with your kind, not since I'm seventeen and on my own. An anticleric's what my Louie used to call me. An honorable appellation, I would say. They've opened up old Galileo's case again. Imagine it. We see it spinning out in space, this Earth, with our own eyes, and so they'll reconsider whether possibly they made a little error back in 1642.

Priscilla finds this very interesting but must get Winnie to the toilet. She tries to pull her panties down and sit her. Hah! cries Winnie, pulling them back up. I won't have any funny business in me panties, thank you very much!

Of course they'd never even have the file on him, if Napoleon's soldiers hadn't sacked the Vatican, says Megan, to no one in particular.

A man in Indiana dials 7667—That's Eulalie—wants to know her favorite color:
    Blue.
    Her favorite dish?
    That's tuna melt. Why is he calling her, a perfect stranger…?
    Research, Madame. It's a research project. Station GVX in Terre Haute, to ascertain if people with the same digits in their phone numbers in different states have any other things in common.
    Has she children?
    One.
    Grandchildren?
    Wait a minute. Who is calling?
    Research, Madame. Play a musical…?
    She doesn't. Number years completed school?
    Eulalie hangs the phone up, mortified. She never reached the sixth.

Mir ist so wunderbar, Megan croons to Billy, hanging upside down.
She wishes she could reproduce the dungeon whispers in *Fidelio.*

Rebecca takes a group from Sunshine Club

to Mini Mart to get some napkins for the
birthday party. Berta Bechtel skips
and Bobby carries a flower that he's picked.

It must be nice in some ways, she thinks,
to be retarded, get such a bang out of a little
walk to the store.

She takes Bobbie's hand at the corner.
It's as soft and trusting as a baby's.

Superstition. You find it everywhere, says Megan. And priests…
From the halls of Monte zu u ma…Berta Bechtel sings and skips
You take Montezuma, Megan says, you take the Aztecs. Montezuma just
collapsed, turned over all he had to What's-his-name…Cortez. Cortez
invited him to wine and women, and he moaned, accepted. It was all
ordained by stars, thought Montezuma…

…to the shores of Tripoli…

Berta Bechtel pushes the traffic button, brings the east and west-bound
traffic to a halt on Main Street,

*Once the Great Road, a busy thoroughfare from earliest times, it was used
by early settlers of Connecticut. It branched south in what is now Weston.
Produce traveled it to Boston, and, in return, came sugar and molasses from
the West Indies. A Bonaparte passed through Waltham on the Great Road in
1804, and James Munroe, in 1817.*

The little group from the Sunshine Club has crossed Nonantum Street,
avoiding The Kisser, who is wearing his Red Sox uniform this morning,
and has just purchased a packet of peanutbutter cups in the Myrtle Spa.
He's on his way to Mass at the French Church. There are some people that
just laugh and allow him to buss them on the lips as he passes. Opinion
about town is that he's harmless, but Rebecca feels that mental health
requires setting certain boundaries, and steers her charges well around
him. He caught her once, as she was coming out of Grover Cronin's. She

looked up and there he…soft and gentle, not what she expected, not a dirty kiss. She takes Bobby's hand to cross the river. Sun's behind a cloud now.

Going to be snow flowers, says Berta Bechtel,
leaning over the railing.

The Kisser pops a Peanutbutter Cup in his mouth and crushes it against his palate, sweet and salty. It's eleven twenty. A parachutist, practicing for the Policemen's Expo, lands in front of the field house at Leary Field.

This date in 1970, a tank of liquid oxygen aboard the Apollo spacecraft, burst three quarters of the way to the moon and forced its return to Earth.

The Kisser…sweet and salty, sweet and salty…spies a pouting…catch her undefending, fresh and sulky adolescent, lanky hair. He crosses, and she disappears in the crowd that's gathering in the Common: Nuclear Disarmament. The evil that I do not want is what I…Gone. He dodges the Number 60 bus, and crosses to the French Church, as they call St. Charles", finds the old broom he's hidden by the rectory shed and sweeps the steps. Who will deliver me…? He picks two paper cups out of the hedge, a vodka bottle, throws them in a trash bag that he carries for the purpose. *Who will deliver me from this body of death?*

He goes in the sanctuary next, and gathers up the Shorter Missal booklets from the back pews and distributes them in the front where the small congregation sits. You needn't. Sister Muriel says, coming in from the convent with the Hosts and a tray of water glasses. He averts his eyes from her lips and continues what he's doing. He's his duties—self-appointed—she has hers.

At the Sunshine Club, they're eating meatloaf, canned peas, and instant mashed, fruit Jello with canned peaches and a dab of Cool Whip.

Priscilla, who's arrived with the two sisters
and seated them at tables, tries to unwind
in her head the processing of this food, to visualize
these peas back in their pods,

potatoes in their
earthy skins, and peaches
in their fuzzy jackets.

She finds it difficult if not impossible. Adie's food, they've blended further into a pap, which she spoons into the gaping toothless mouth.

Yes, spring's expected to be late and cold, says Henrietta Rose—a rather elegant lady felled by drink—to her tablemates. It has to do with some volcano down in Mexico, I hear… The hell you say, growls Terry Fratus. and Adie licks the mashed potatoes from her fingers.

Hardly scintillating dinner conversation, thinks Henrietta. She recalls the dinners that she used to hostess…Henrietta's extravaganzas, people called them, there on that plateau of Sogamoso…
dusky little wives of her husband's underling engineers…the waiters in and out with appetizers, children underfoot in nighties…barman, who had had a few himself just after midnight,
beginning to improvise a *copla* that would last till three.

They'd find him in the morning stretched across
the front seat of the guitarist's taxi in the drive,
the rest of the *conjunto* sleeping under
the great ceiba hung with orchids in
their baskets…Oh it was lovely.

It was the dusky little wives that exercised her hostess faculties,
the beautiful, dark women with their oily perspiration, their silences.
They'd only talk of servants, babies…

Apple cake! says Adie, gabbling the mash.

Yes, quite a partygiver, I was once,
says Henrietta to Priscilla. I don't know where it went,
sometimes, where I lost it all, the children
in their nighties, the rambling house, so lovely.
The clouds would lift; we'd see the *páramo*.

All pink it was sometimes.

Babbling woman, says Terry.
You might be civil!
Hell, you say.
I will simply ignore you. Henrietta turns to Alva Otting.

It's a lovely meatloaf, Alva, won't you eat?
I wanted catsup, Alva whines.
You might have asked, says Henrietta, passing it.

An old rag bundle, just an old rag bundle. Why should anybody bother?
Everything, they took away, my house, they took…

Too bad, says Henrietta. I feel that way about…of no great value really…
pots, my baskets from the Amazon…they moved with me, three continents,
and still I have them…a little cannon that I found in the grass in San Mateo,
where Bolívar…

Hell, you say.
I will ignore your rudeness

…a bit of grapeshot
that I dug out of an old door. More than
a century ago, that war, and everything
as if it happened yesterday.

It wasn't open to the public, I recall; we bribed a workman with a bottle of
Ron Viejo…

Rum, she drank, those days, a cheap dark brand of Ron de Caldas; she
recalls they bottled it in the same bottles as the purgative they made for
cattle. She took to drinking it a day after, horrified, she saw she'd downed
in fifteen minutes a bottle of Gran Marnier that took forty years to age…

Aguardiente, she came down to next. Six pesos for a liter and the next
worst thing to the cattle purge.

I lived on Squires Court Road and owned my house, says Alva. I had the Polish grocers one block down, the Russian Church and…

What a conversation, growls Terry Fratus.

Well, it's better than a sullen silence, Henrietta says, and Priscilla, mopping up Adie's plate, thinks she's rather heroic.

Was that when? Henrietta wonders, was the aguardiente when? They moved to India soon after. More dusky wives, her husband's engineers. She left them now—their talk of servants, babies—to their own devices; and discovered *bwana bap*, the people's drink. two rupies the half gallon…

Have you children? Henrietta asks Priscilla, noting her milky skin, the small patch of adolescent acne healed beside her brow, the bitten nails and mannish haircut. But she has nice brown eyes and a womanly shape—she could be pretty if she cared for herself.

I have three, Priscilla says.
An air of breeding too. Henrietta can always pick that up.
Notice them, she says. I didn't notice mine and I regret it.
I'll try to, Priscilla says, thinking again of the hickey on Solie's neck.

A second parachutist lands in Leary Field before a gathered crowd of mothers, infants in their strollers. Father Tours begins the Mass at the French Church. Eulalie Arsenault—who's hidden Alcide's walk-aid at a neighbor's—and The Kisser seated at the front, loud with responses. Eulalie mumbles hers in French. She's already devising a way to avoid him going out. There's also Megan Blakey's brother Leo, several French Canadians related to Eulalie, and a scattering of ladies of the Holy Name,

A good man, Leo, thinks Eulalie, comes to see his sisters every day, and all of them good Catholics, with the exception of that Megan.

Therefore it is with Angels and Archangels, Thrones and Dominations…

Henrietta is going to perform a piece by Brahms on her harp as soon as the Mayor arrives. Priscilla tells Megan about it in hopes of perking her up.

Brahms, you say?

Yes, would you like to meet her?

No, the music will suffice. My Louie and I used go to concerts every month. We would have gone more if we could. He played the oboe in one of Roosevelt's orchestras, and only earned a pittance for many years, so there never was much money, but we entertained ourselves. We went on lovely walks and recited the lyrics of Sir William Gilbert to each other. He was knighted, did you know…

We will walk down Picadilly with a poppy or a lily…

Ah, yes, there was always music. We were rich in music. The symphony cost fifty cents, and even that a sacrifice. We heard the Greats, yes, Charles Munch, and Rudolf Serkin. Louie worshipped ground he…I remember, later, hearing Peter, Peter Serkin, Rudolf's son you know…had the effrontery to appear once in a pair of old brown shoes. Imagine it! Imagine it! A little difference with his father, we heard later. A little difference with the world, his generation. Well, my Louie wouldn't clap. He was incensed, of course; and then one heard he'd thrown it over, Peter, all the work, the discipline. What did Papa Rudolf think, one wonders? Yes, music was a holy thing to us. I hear he straightened out though, Peter.

Eulalie Takes the Host and Flees the Kisser

Eulalie takes the host on her tongue from Father Tours, returns to a seat near the choir door to avoid The Kisser, who has taken the Host in the palm of his hand, denying himself oral pleasure in this setting. The final blessing and Eulalie slips out the back way where a hearse is arriving for the funeral Mass to follow: One of the numerous Aucoins, Armand; he owned a machine shop—stamping, drilling—was married into a flock of Robichauds, the Nova Scotia, not the Acadian ones. She goes around the back to reach the convenience store on the corner of Main and Regis Court, there buys a Megabucks and puts her telephone number, in case it was a sign—that man calling from Indiana.

The Kisser notes Eulalie fleeing. Sooner would he kiss a mackerel than that woman.

He tastes the little papery Host becoming
Our Lord's Body as it passes his tongue
and down his chastened...
           He's left the church by west door, lopes back toward
The Common, where he waits at railroad crossing
foot of Moody for the Boston & Main to pass.
One-fifty-eight. It's thirteen minutes late.
           The husky girl in mountaineering boots
emerges from her little house to wave her flag.
He glimpses pouting black girl on the other side
The train pulls through. He loses sight of her,
but here she is again in front of him.
           Sullen puss in tight pink dress.
Pouting rosebud...Rosa Mundo.
But his heart is pure...
           Oh, no you don't! Not at my crossing! yells
the husky girl in boots. *Her* crossing! And
she's going to strike him with her flag it seems!
He skitters sideways, but she catches him on
his neck and shoulders, she's not having any
funny business at her crossing!

And so, redeemed, he passes on, around the Bay Bank on the corner, up Moody Street where Rosa is hurrying past Grover Cronin's, on the way to pick up her schedule from the agency, doesn't see him till he's almost… hasn't time to cross the…Well, it's quicker, let him…let it…and he kisses her quite gently on the mouth. His soft dog's eyes look into hers, and she laughs and hurries on. Nut capital of the world, she thinks, this town. Her lips retain an impress of softness. Quite a nice man, really, she thinks. He's always clean and nicely dressed in one of his uniforms—he has several, including a military one with medals. She often sees him sweeping the steps in front of the French Church.

Eulalie, on her way home through the Mount Peake Cemetery, stops at her favorite place, a grave of rough pink granite on a little spit of land that juts into the river where it's widest. A plaque reads

ANNE HATHAWAY ABBOT
SHE WAS, ABOVE ALL THINGS, GLAD AND YOUNG
1945-1975

Barely thirty. Shame.

THE DAUGHTERS OF POTATO FAMINE
STAGE SIXTH ANNUAL LUNCHEON…
reads the sign around the Shawmut Bank.

It's two o'clock, and they're still waiting for the Mayor at The Sunshine Club. They make some Easter bunnies out of felt, for decorations meanwhile. The Easter Bunny's dead, the real one, Bertha Bechtel says. When I was younger, at The Children's Own, he was alive. He brought me, once, a doll with curls and little holsters with pistols.

Eulalie's climbed the little rise across from *Le Watch*,
as the French Canadians called the old watch factory.
She's following the Aucoin funeral.
A wash of green is over the early leafing willows…
grabs her heart right out of her chest.
The beeches are coming out in copper too.

Thence they came to another high-pointed rock having a fair ascent on the west side which they called Mount Feake, from one Robert Feake who had

married the Governour's daughter

Governour Winthrop

The hearse has disappeared behind a rise. Aucoins will be at the farthest end. Eulalie marvels they got in at all. Acadian Aucoins. They came here victims like her own of

> *Le Grand Derangement*: the broken families…
> twelve of them, Eulalie's, distributed
> as public charges in surrounding towns—
> three here, four there; her grandfather, Theo, wandering
> deranged in search of his lost children.

PLASTIC FLOWERS ARE PERMITTED ONLY IN OCTOBER THRU MAY CYCLISTS AND PICNICKERS PROHIBITED

Is posted on an ancient beech tree. Eulalie sits to get her breath among the Weekses: Nahum, Father; Minnie Mae, Beloved Mother. Daughters, Lucy and Mabel lie under smaller stones. We Will Meet in Heaven…

Jose Maso on WHYY spins *Cuando Tu Te Hayas Ido,* for Concha from Ambrosio. It's almost three o'clock, and Alcide's napping, dreaming of Antoinette Fandel, the little girl that comes in to help Eulalie Mondays, cleans the oven, swabs the floors. She tells him that she's pregnant. Zut! He should have known he'd get her into trouble dreaming of her constantly! Fresh. She can't be more than fourteen; you only have to look at them, their bellies swell, those fresh ones.

Farwell, Moody, Jellison… Eulalie
climbs through Yankee ghosts.
Fiore, Lawyer—they didn't used to let
Italians in here—with a lovely sandstone angel
standing over him. Pages, mother, father, little one
that lived a month. The Roberts Family grandly
gathered round a mausoleum, fenced in with iron spikes.

She trespasses among them, pondering mortality; then climbs.
Swedes here, Isaakson, Borg, Helsingius, Oscar—worked at *Le Watch*.
They called him Snowball. Kept to themselves
and had their chapel there on River Street.
Always had the best jobs at *Le Watch*.

She caught her hair once in the machine they had
for buffing pinions. It was Snowball freed her,
scolded, comforted. She moves among her own now
at the furthest end. It doesn't even look like cemetery here,
but like some raw new housing development.

Labbe, Lebrun, Langille…*Le Grand Derangement.*
They sent her grandfather in chains to Cuba, where he escaped
and stowed below the deck on a ship to New Orleans.
He lived on water and sardines for three months.
Wasn't sure where he was when he emerged,
had to ask two people was this New Orleans?
before he believed.

Ah, here's the hearse, the gash, the pile of red earth.
Eulalie watches as they lower the late
Armand Aucoin to final rest.

Rosa returns to the Sunshine Club to check on Wolfie. Rebecca is handing
out juice and cookies, and Mrs. Rose is telling the group that a spaceship
called Columbia is in orbit today and just passing over Africa. At least this
is something more interesting for Wolfie than what is the next holiday
coming. He probably has all different holidays anyway. She knows Jews
do. She puts his chair next to Mrs. Rose, who sometimes performs on her
harp, and who, Rosa knows instinctively, is a person Wolfie would like to
talk to if he could. Stupid Adie Blakey, whose legs are apart in her geriatric
chair so that you can see way up to her diaper, asks Rebecca if she is Adie's
mother. Adie calls for her mother all day long.
    Innerspring,
says Adie's sister Winnie, who is *tonto* in a different way than Adie, and
who no one likes. Rosa wonders what that word means. Innerspring. She's

never heard it.

Eulalie's home, takes off her shoes, and Alcide wakes from his dream of the little girl he's made pregnant. He'll have to marry her, of course, he thinks. He'll find the money somewhere… He's out of bed and searching for his walk-aid.

It isn't in any of Eulalie's customary hiding places: cellar landing, laundry room…a…job…some money…breathing hard. He found it this morning stuck on the shelf above the coats in the hall closet. Of course it won't be there now. There's still a chance, of course, that she's not in a family way… he hasn't touched her, only dreamed. And possibly she doesn't bleed yet. Just a kid, but they bleed early now. He makes his way down the hall, sees Eulalie in her EZBoy. Eulalie hasn't bled last twenty years; he wonders does Melissa at the Press Box still? That Rosa that comes to bathe him, he would wager she…

The Mayor is late, so Rosa goes upstairs to change her flooded pad and make Wolfie's bed. They did it in the bed once. He wanted so bad to try, "the normal way." She got him in there somehow. Lay on top of him, but nothing happened. It was something that needed to happen just the way it happened, without all the planning and the wanting to be like other people, she concluded, and she guessed Wolfie did too, for he never asked for it again.

She crosses the sluicegate again, feels her blood gushing out of her just like the dammed up river water. Wofie has undammed me, thinks. Maybe it won't last a month this time. She's ten minutes late for Alcide's bath when she enters the yellow brick building at the foot of Crescent Street, wonders if they've found him.

He's there. He was brought home by police, Eulalie tells her, for shitting in the gutter on Moody Street. He probably just needed to badly, Rosa says. Men in her village did this very neatly all the time.

Well it's the second time, and I was very upset. She is calming herself with the horoscope from *The Globe*. It's telling her to focus on "extra earnings," she says. She's going to get a job so she can put Alcide away. She can't tolerate him any longer.

She probably could get a job, thinks Rosa, watching Eulalie's energetic legs as she crosses and recrosses them, concentrating on the horoscope. And she's legal for the past sixty years at least. Do the French just come over the border without anyone bothering them? It seems so. Eulalie told her once how she used to work at the mill, when it was a mill, not apartments for *ancianos*, and come home every night and cry for the farm in Canada, where they kept sheep and wove their own blankets.

But there wasn't enough food for so many children,
so half of them had to come here and live in a little room on Cherry Street
and wash their stockings in the bathroom sink and work
six days a week cleaning the lint from under the looms.

But they had schools and English lessons and clubs, Eulalie told her, not like now, when you can go to the adult education at the High School if you have the money and aren't afraid of being turned in for illegal…

She has a soft spot for Eulalie since she told Rosa these things. Still, she could never shame a man the way Eulalie does.

I hid it at the top of the closet, this time, Eulalie says. "I can no imageen how he find it. Rosa laughs and passes another clot. Eulalie hasn't bled for fifteen years, Alcide told her once in the bath. As if that put her past his interest. He never put his hand up Rosa's skirts, in any case, and she doubts she'd let him. He just likes to *think* about women, she concludes. What they might be like if he had them. Probably he imagines everything, just like the job he thinks they're offering him at the used car place. A job, they tell him. You meet the public. He keeps going back to hear it over and over. Eulalie, on the other hand, could get a job. Eulalie was probably good looking in her day, she thinks.

Innerspring. The word pops in her head. What it mean, innerspring? she asks Eulalie.
    It's the bottom part of the bed, Eulalie says. With the springs in it.

Rosa feels a fool and vaguely disappointed. Of course, Eulalie knows things she doesn't know, the French being better schooled than the Hondurans and all that bunch. Probably there weren't so many of them all at once, coming in. And there was the mill that needed them, and the watch factory, where Eulalie worked after her first job at the mill.

Too many of us, she thinks. Alcide told her once how he loved the pigeons that he fed in the park. They are really very beautiful" he told her. If you look closely at them. It's just there are too many of them.

Too many of us, yes, she thinks. This thought always brings an image of the Guatemalans downstairs, flooding the toilet, clogging the washing machine, taking apart their cars in the yard. Fortunately they were Laureano's worry. She would come home and find the toilet pulled up by its roots and the washing machine set out to the trash and one of the spare ones in the yard installed.

It seems, says Eulalie, some woman's little girl saw him about his dirty business, and screamed, and the police came and brought him home. They would have taken him in if Officer Menard who's married to my cousin, Ottilie Rosier hadn't been one of them. So they bring him to me. Going to have to watch him better they tell me. 'We should have booked him.'

Book him, I scream at them. Go right ahead. Maybe they send him off somewhere! I've had my fill. *Dieu*! Man that can't keep his pants on…

Alcide is docile and exhausted. She gives him a sponge bath, as he says he's too weak to get in the tub. He's grateful and leans up against her like a little boy while she sponges him off seated on the toilet. You've missed the Sunshine Club, she tells him. They're having a birthday party for Adie Blakey and the Mayor's coming.

Ah, well, I have to tend to my affairs, says Alcide. It's no small thing when you get a young thing pregnant.

What young thing? asks Rosa, shocked.
What's Her Name, that comes to clean.

Oh, he means the little girl that Eulalie hired for after school, to mop the floors.

But she can't be. She's only eleven or so…

She bleeds. You just have to look at those young ones to knock them up.

That's probably what he did, Rosa thinks, *looked* at her.

You can still go if you want. Get your mind off things, she tells him.

Sunshine Club? *Pas.* What kind of a club is that? In my day we had real clubs:

French American Athletic and Literary Club. That was a propaire club.

What you do?

We recited poetry. Racine, we recited. By memory. Then we played quoits.

That sound nice. Maybe you give them some ideas like that. Some intelligent people go there. Mr. Wolfe was a famous lawyer once. And Mrs. Rose has lived in every country in the world, they say. I'll bet she knows some poetry.

> *Merde,* he says, leaning his head against her flank and closing his eyes.
> *Mierda,* she says in her own idiom, and laughs.
> *Que se vayan todos a la mierda!*

She dries him off. He has a healthy red sex. Probably did very well in its time. It's best to have it all in his head at this time of life, though she probably wouldn't say the same for Wolfie. They are all different, she thinks, marveling. On one of her soap operas, there's a man who comes back from war and passes for another soldier who was killed. Fools the whole town, even the man's wife. She disbelieves it. She knows there are no two people enough alike in the whole world to fool anyone. Pigeons were another matter. Not even Guatemalans were close to being as alike as pigeons.

Let's go, she says. She wants to see the party, and the Mayor.

He lets her push him in the chair, across again to The Mill. Poor man. She ought to let him rest, but Eulalie needs a rest too. She finds a place for him next to Adie. He looks very nice, she thinks. She's combed his hair straight back and straightened out the earpieces of his glasses.

Am I alive? cries Adie, waking from a little nap in her chair.

Rosa gravely takes her pulse. Yes, you are Adie. I can feel your heart. You don't want to die today.

The Mayor hasn't arrived and Mrs. Rose is filling up the time with music on her harp. It is turning out a nice day. Priscilla is sitting with Megan Blakey—the one sister who is in her right mind—who is telling everyone in a loud voice how, unlike others of her race, she was able to have only one child:

Coitus interruptus, that's how. If ever any of them read a book that wasn't prescribed by the Pope they'd have known! Megan hates the priests and the Church. It's shocking to Rosa.

Where she comes from it's the men who hate the Church, never the women. And never would a woman wish for only one child, and such a one as Megan's daughter who has never even come to see her, and who's out in California smoking pot. Even Laureano, who says he hates priests, wanted her to call for Father Artemio that time he fell off the roof and broke his head....

Ah, but it's bad luck to even think such a thought.... She breaks off to remind the Virgin of her petition for Laureano not to fall off the ladder today.

Not today. She feels faint from loss of blood and lack of lunch, and asks Priscilla to watch Alcide a minute while she goes to drink some Cool Aid. She thought they'd be cutting the cake by now. The Mayor is more than an hour late, Rebecca complains.

Berta Bechtel, clutching her patent leather pocketbook to her breast, sings the Marine Hymn through two times, and Megan tells Henrietta Rose how the Church, she reads, has opened up the case of Galileo to reconsider if possibly they made

A little blunder back in 1542.

The Mayor's Come

The Mayor's come, The Honorable Arthur Clark.

They bring the cake, with ten candles to blow out. Adie doesn't understand what's wanted, so Rebecca blows them out. I made a wish you'll live another bunch of years, she tells Adie

I'd shoot myself first, says Megan. Doesn't even know that she's alive. Another bunch of years indeed!

Megan told Rosa once that if she had the use of her legs she'd kill them both. No good to tell her it's a sin.

The Mayor stands to make a speech now. He talks about Adie's birthday, and the coming birthday of the city, and about the spaceship Columbia going round and round overhead, and how this is the same date in April as the first space flight of Yuri Somebody of Russia in the spaceship Vostok.

Rosa is moved by this special day. It is a fine speech, and reminds her of a man from her village who used to speak on special occasions, all in rhyme. He could just stand up on his legs, without thinking about it ahead of time or writing it down, and say it all in rhyme.

Only an hour till the van comes and the party's over. Rebecca starts to clean up the colored paper and felt markers. Berta Bechtel tells Rosa the Easter Bunny's dead. When I lived at the Children's Own, he was alive. He brought me once a little doll with curls and little holster with real pistols. Rebecca lets this go again without bringing in Reality, and praises Bobby Rosier for coloring within the lines. Henrietta tells Ada a story about a ride she had once on an elephant. Ada's asleep, but Rosa can tell from Wolfie's intelligent eyes that he's listening and would like to push some words out of his own.

The Mayor comes around now, shaking hands. Rosa has her turn, and starts to blush, thinking how maybe he can see that she's illegal. She falls into another of her imaginings of how Wolfie, if he could, would make Laureano marry her for all her caring for him all these years and nursing him after all his accidents. She feels low when she thinks about this problem. Like those Haitians who walk up Moody Street asking passersby to marry them. One young man even asked her once. Marry me won't do you no good, she told him. Well, then maybe you got a daughter legal? I got a daughter in the army, she told him. And she doesn't want to marry you.

They just smile and stop the next woman they see. No pride left. She has
pride, yes.

A black and white feline, presents himself as stray at the door, is let in
by Albert, who takes it on his lap; and, grinning, strokes him, infuriating
Henrietta Rose, who cannot bear his baseless mirths, the self-sufficiency of
his pleasures.
    Obfuscation! Winnie roars. Objurgation!
    Chloroform them if I could, says Megan, pleased at shocking Rebecca.
    Lovey Mother, cries Adie, overtired, picking at her cake and ice cream
    Unnatural acts with animals, thinks Henrietta, watching Albert.

Berta is to sing once more and she, to play. Priscilla, meanwhile is in the
bathroom wrestling with Winnie's panties. She has a stiff-armed way of
opposing you that's highly effective Priscilla's found.
    Help! she cries, in concert with Berta's warbling.
    …*twas there that I firsmet sweemolly Ballone…*
Berta Bechtel, whose singing is much made over, hasn't anybody, never
had. Her unknown mother bore her in an insane asylum, and they sent her
to some foster parents after, kept her seven years. She went to school and
learned to read, but started acting funny, so they put her in the Fernald
School for Imbeciles.

She got out at eighteen, and there was
a man she was to marry. An ice truck
ran him over and he died before her eyes.

It sent her simple. But someone, somewhere
must have loved her, sometime; she's so good,
Rebecca, who has theories, thinks.

Winnie passes a stool resembling a blackberry.
And Henrietta Rose, her rouged old cheeks aflame, is next,
performing *Liebestraum* upon her harp.

Lovey Mother, Adie wails.
The Honorable Arthur Clark is studying

a place where Albert put his fist
right through the wallboard.

Chloroform them if I could…

They never enjoy these birthday parties, Rebecca thinks.
Well Bertha does, and Bobby. And Megan has enjoyed the…
After the Liebestraum, she requests something by Brahms,
which Henrietta is able to provide: one of the intermezzos
arranged for harp that's stored in some part of her memory
unaffected by the alcohol damage she's suffered—the Korsakoff's
that will cause her, by this evening, to forget this whole event.

The harp's an instrument I wouldn't have chosen myself, Henrietta tells
Priscilla when she comes back to the table; but my mother thought it
ladylike. Wouldn't have her daughter playing horns or big bosomed viols,
or tucking dirty napkins under her chin and contorting herself to play a
fiddle. I think I would have liked the cello.

Oh, I too, Priscilla says. Henrietta notes the grammar of her reply. A well
bred girl, just as she thought. Yes, gently bred, Priscilla is, and liberally
educated. She keeps it pretty much a secret. That is since her sophomore year
at Mount Holyoke when she dropped out to participate in an occupation of
the projected site of the Seabrook Power Plant, and to have Solie.

She and Solie's father lived downtown behind the library, and Solie slept
in a bureau drawer under a poster with Mario Savio's words in large red
letters:

*There is a time when the operation of the machine becomes so
odious you've got to put your bodies on the gears and upon the
wheels to indicate to the people who run it that, unless you're free,
the machines will be prevented from working at all.*

She didn't actually put her body on the growing reactor. Other people did
that. She and David and the others who formed their group that met in
the basement of the Congregational Church were the supply team, who

brought food and water and clean clothing in to the campers inside the facility. David, who was still hanging in with his studies at Brandeis, was their trainer, for there was great physical strength and skill required for their work. At night they practiced wire cutting and knots: Figure eights,

Butterflly,
Prusick,
Double fisherman's.
And in the day, they went to an abandoned playground behind the Banks Street School to practice
Texas High Kick,
Prusick,
Tree Stirrup,
Low Anchor.

Because of Solie, her work was mostly shopping and preparing cartons of supplies in the basement of the church: but she did go over the fence once, using the inch-worm method because she was carrying a heavy load of dried beans and powdered milk. Sitting on the upper ascender with her feet on the lower she inched up at dusk one February night, using the rocking motion she'd practiced at the playground, cutting the barbed wire at the top, and then inching down. She wasn't seen; there was never any danger until she was over and saw a flashlight from a quarter opposite the area occupied by the campers. So she hid in the bushes for several hours, fearing dogs. She was still nursing Solie then, so her breasts flooded with milk. She'd brought a hand pump and occupied herself emptying the milk, discarding it on the ground and drinking some of it herself, she became so hungry before the campers finally found her and gave her coffee and helped her back over.

Eventually David ended up inside, and she went on marches with Solie on her back and sat in jail once for five days while Mrs Osorio next door watched Solie. Sharing a tent on Boston Common with Ross Pfister, who ran the business end of their enterprise, she ended up pregnant with Frostie. This sobered Ross, it seemed forever, and they married the year the first reactor started going up. She didn't see her family at all during this time, for which her mother still hasn't forgiven her. It wasn't so much

Rowans she was rejecting, for they were a varied lot, including a number of eccentrics and even criminals. But Gideon Rowan had married Rika Madsen, daughter of a Swedish foreman at The Watch. And Rika had a stricter notion than any Rowan ever had of what was required of and due a Rowan. Priscilla supposes it was these notions she was rejecting. And it was a time of trying out new notions of what one's life path might be. David, for example, who came of a long line of lawyers, eventually left Brandeis to apprentice himself at the glass blowing works downtown.

Young and Crippen are talking to the Vice President—the President is still at the White House convalescing from an assassin's bullet. Romania has expelled the British envoy…crackdown foreseen this year on acid rain…Two bodies have been found in the Merrimack River.

The cat with the appointment leaps down from Albert's lap and heads for the door. He belongs to a woman who pushes him in a supermarket cart on top of a pile of old clothing. Her name is Helen Schade and she has been released from the Metropolitan State Hospital for almost a year and rents a little room with hotplate, share a bath on Myrtle Street. The feline finds his Mistress on Norumbega Street. She's on her way to a yard sale out at Piety Corner. Well, jump in, you ingrate, had yourself an adventure, did you? Well jump. I'm not going to stoop and pick you up, don't think it.

Hey you Cat Lady, the Maggot calls. He's curled around a bottle of Lambrusco on the river bank. The Professor sits above him with a finger raised. Cats won't ask you, Madame, what's the meaning of it all. No, man asks, Madame. Have you heard of Sigmund Freud? She hurries on. She doesn't know this Sigmund, and cannot understand how anyone can live like these two without a little place—with hotplate, share a bath—to call their own. The Purpose, madam, of this life is, simply speaking, nothing more than the Pleasure Principle. That man ought to be happy, Madam, to be sure, is not included in the plan, dear lady, of Creation.

She pushes her cart over the bridge. They found a body here once.

…happiness only possible as episodic…prolonged, produces nothing more than feeling of mild contentment. Goethe warns us nothing is as hard to bear as a succession of fair days, he calls after her.

It's disgraceful, thinks Helen Schade. It used to be that you could walk home, an afternoon, undisturbed. She doesn't know what's happened to this town. She stops to catch her breath, and watches an MDC launch pass below. Will it be a body? She remembers February past, the girl that floated after the thaw, near Roberts. Pregnant, they said she was. The launch is nosing in the weeds near pilings where Nutting's Ballroom used to be… Find that professor dead, one of these days, for all his fancy talk.

Drowned, or electrocuted, like that one
last year that pissed the third rail of the trestle.

…though, har, that may of course be an exaggeration, The Professor finishes, kicking The Maggot.

An English Lesson

Four o'clock. They line up for the minivan at the Sunshine club. Rebecca helps Priscilla with the three fretful sisters. Margo's come, the evening girl. She pours the sixteen ounces of Sparkling Rose that Megan gets on her shift.

On her bike then, and hurrying to her other job at the Service Center on Charles Street,

Jesús Roldán is absent. Antonia says he's sick today:

Oh, bad, is bad, oh, missus, cold is cold y *suda*. He sweat and is cold at same time.

And leg don't heal. And he not eat. I make him all the thing he love.

Not sweets. You must not give him sweets.

Que puedo yo? I say him no, but he is want sometimes .

She sits and drinks the boiled and reboiled Café Bustelos that they've made, a guava tart that Antonia's bought at the Chinese grocers.

Do you test him?

Yes, Missus. It turn pink.

That means sugar. No sweets. He must not have the sweets. What else?

Conchita has the toothache. Concha shows her an upper molar.

You call Dr Vurgopolis. Tell him pain, *dolor*.

Pain.

Goes on and on?

No, Missus, *como un cuchillo*…

Like a knife. You tell him. And tell him he promised you can make the payments

monthly.

Payments. Monthly.

She asks them the question from the English book.

Where are you from?

What do you do?

Antonia was born in Aguadillas on Puerto Rico's western coast.

What does she do?

A housewife, Missus, *que mas va a*…?

Concha is from Aguadillas also. She's a housewife also.

Ana Gil's from Cochabamba, Ecuador.

She doesn't mention what she does, and no one asks.

She entertains men overnight for large sums. Dr. Vurgopolis is among them and all her dental work

Antonia's children come in from school. They are beautiful children, and sit down at another table to do their homework. Antonia forbids them to play in the street. Only the oldest is allowed to play baseball with Los Padres.

What did their fathers do?

What did they did, Missus?

No, What did they do. The auxiliary tells you it's past tense, Priscilla explains.

Pero, 'do'…

Ah, *did, do.* The English language is difficult to explain. One is the auxiliary, and one…

Only Antonia nods in understanding.

Antonia's father was a country teacher. Concha never knew her father. Nor did Ana Gil.

Ana's mother took in washing from the great houses, washed the sheets in the Rio Cochabamba and stretched them on the banks in the sun to bleach. Ana didn't want her mother's life; she got away soon as she could.

A paper cup! You bring me wine in a paper cup! cries Megan.

Adie, overtired, throws her gifts off the tray of her geriatric chair: a little bottle of Jean Nate from Becky, a yellow incense candle from Henrietta Rose, a Snoopy pin from Bobby.

Margo brings back the wine back in a tumbler. She needs to ask if Megan's had a BM today.

You're blushing! Megan hoots at her. Every time you ask me that, you blush. A bowel movement. It's a natural phenomenon. Where'd we be if we didn't move them? All this whispering about and blushing! Bring it in the open, girlie! Death, decomposition. Natural things!

Margo carries her burning face to Adie's room and straightens the bureau blindly, noting the letter from the President and Mrs. Reagan, greeting Adie on her hundredth… Why?

Why don't they die. Why don't they die and let us live? There's something owed the young, too, after all!

Oh, what is wrong with me? It's no use blaming them. You got into this by yourself, girlie. They didn't make you throw away your education.

Why don't I die? frets Adie.
And Megan's turned her radio to one of Chopin's rueful, stumbling mazurkas.

No, it wasn't them that made you throw away your education. You did it all yourself.
She's in her second year of nursing, Margo; and also in her first trimester.

Lima beans, Priscilla says.
habas de las Indias
They're gandules, Ana says, in Ecuador.
Alberjas, zanahorias. Peas and carrots.
Banana, *banano.*
Plátano, plantain.

When she was shopping for the Occupiers, she used to buy plátanos at the market, thinking they were bananas. The latinos in the market called her, *La señora* who buys *plátano* for bananas. She studied Spanish at the Adult Education then, with Sr. Hugo, who was a Cuban refugee and a spectacularly handsome and elegant man. Castro's Cuba was not for him. They were good friends, though she disagreed with his politics and he with her scruffy life. To him Spanish was the language of Cervantes, and to her an entry into the neighborhood she and David shared on Spring Street with the Mexicans who had the market and the Colombians who lived below them. She used to watch his hands with fascination, and the twitching of his little moustache. Soledad, solitude, he told her, was a beautiful word. She named the baby Soledad, Her mother hated the name, and now Solie hates it too.

Inagotable, another beautiful word she remembers from those days. It meant inexhaustible.

Agotar meant to wear away drop by drop. She can still recall the graceful little gestures with which he illustrated the little drops, *gotas*…

The *plátano* is longer, says Antonia, and its skin is thicker.

An Apparition on Moody Street

The Kisser lopes home. He's sated with the liftings up
and castings down of the day. He's cursed, he thinks.
He sees a glory no one else…
He thinks of Rosa. She told him, once,
her name, one of her gifts. And she allowed
his kiss. Twice.

Today she laughed. She laughed,
she laughed and spread wide her body to a blessing.
Rosa. Rosa Mundo. He smelled her earth smell,
generative juices. Fecundated not by him.
His kiss was chaste. His kisses always chaste
as he recalls them. But only she allows, vouchsafes,
receives them as he gives them.
Laughs, like that ancient Sarah.

    A Negress, tall, she must be seven feet,
    skates past him, right up the middle of Moody Street,
    she strides on wheels, and disappears below
    the rise. A queenly figure, hair piled upon
    her head and bound in an exotic scarf
    that flows behind.

    An apparition? No, he catches the look
    of disapproval on the face of an
    old black woman carrying two shopping bags,
    and disbelief on other faces… Some one whistles.

    Back, she comes now, over the summit.
    The low sun lights her blackness from behind.
    The largest life that's ever been seen
    on Moody Street, and he isn't
    the only one to see it.

    It's offered to all, because of him.
    She's almost upon him now, her waist nipped in
    above the briefest scarlet skirt.

Regally she glides, her left skate lifted, eyes
the hardest onyx, past him: Who do you think
you're kidding,
Jerk Off!

*Young and Crippen are turning somersaults in the cabin, and having a light
snack. One of the power units is running a low temp; but not a matter for
concern.*

What Priscilla Needed

They're having a conference on Nelson Márquez at the Service Center. A system of rewards, says Mr. Jones, the Baptist minister who runs the place. He shows Priscilla a book he's reading about a man who trained a seal with cookies. Reinforcers, they are called. He wants to make a list of reinforcers for Nelson, and he's numbered on the blackboard, one to ten.

He can go with me for donuts, Carmen, the receptionist suggests. She loves Nelson. That's good, says Mr. Jones. How many points? Oh, ten, Priscilla says, impatient with all this. She's had too many failures. And how will he earn points? He'll learn to read ten syllables, she says. She's given up on words. Out the window of Mr. Jones's office she sees Nelson skirting the flank of St. Charles's Church. Is it a rock he has in his hand? She can't watch, gets herself a cup of tea.

She started working here back in the days of the nine room house in Weston, acre and a half of grass, two Volvos, husband and three children, dog and cat with pedigrees. One day it turned to ashes. A day like this in early spring, Priscilla standing at the kitchen sink...
How had it happened?

After the battle seemed to be lost and the first reactor scheduled to open in a year, Ross quit the project and took his administrative and accounting skills to Arthur D. Little, where he was totally successful and totally fulfilled by solving such problems as why banks needed so many workers to process checks, and why this processing couldn't be accomplished by three-thirty each afternoon so the whole place could close and go home with the tellers.

Frostie had been born, and she was expecting Benno.. Her parents visited and presented them with rugs and dryers and electric knives and all the little appliances that crowded her counter and which she never used, so that she had requested that henceforth her father should give her nothing that had been invented after the stone age. Her only link with the reactor days was Sr. Hugo, who still came to give her classes, and David's appearance now and then to take Solie to the zoo or to the science museum.

By then David was making and selling glass jewelry in
Haymarket and teaching himself classical guitar while working as a security guard at night.

Solie firmly held to Ross as being her father and liked to consider David as just a family friend. She convinced her actual father to take Frostie along on the outings, and soon Frostie and David were like father and son. So, they were all happy except for her, and she ought to have been happy in that beautiful neighborhood with its large groomed lots and brand new houses with four bedrooms and two and a half baths and family rooms as big as their apartment on Spring Street used to be. She walked around it pushing Benno in his stroller and thought it a terribly deprived environment. There was nothing at all to see. No children, no playgrounds, no stores, no animals— well there was a rabbit in a cage they used to visit, but a servant came out to ask them not to come as they were setting off some kind of security device. She took to going into town and taking them on the train one stop down the line to Waltham Common, where they watched the buses and the trains pull in and out, the demonstrators, and the madmen standing on the benches and delivering orations, the people from the halfway houses walking to the store, And eventually she made her way to Spring Street and to Mrs. Osorio.But it wasn't enough. She didn't belong any longer.

And then the first reactor opened.

And then there was Three Mile Island. That was the time of her great fight with Ross:

> You never cared!

> You never really foresaw what could happen to the ocean. To the people downwind…

> It was all just one of your problems, like making it so banks can close earlier.

In a way, it was, he admitted.

Even David, with his hopes of a concert at Carnegie Hall, didn't seem to care. David was becoming crazy.

She went to hear him play at the deCordova Museum and, unhappy with his performance, he threw his best guitar off a precipice. She couldn't believe it, looking down into a brush filled gully and seeing his best guitar at the bottom. Later he admitted it was only his second best guitar.

And so it turned to ashes.
It turned to ashes and that day at the kitchen sink,
she picked up one of the Sheffield knives her father had supplied
in place of the electric one—they weren't quite stone age, but closer than electric;
and she slashed across her wrist, again, again, until Solie came in
and started screaming, and she bound herself up and tried to hide
what she had done, but Solie told Ross.

But why? Why? they asked her: husband, father,
psychiatrist. Why?
She couldn't say.
She sat at McLean Hospital a month enduring all this questioning, but
only, one night alone in the dormitory at Metropolitan State—they sent
her there because she was uncooperative
and didn't appreciate all the amenities and freedoms of McLean—
did she answer the question for herself.

There, in those spartan surroundings, following the Haitian
attendants with their dangling keys, along
the corridors with their great steel doors and deep
barred windows: to the baths, the clinics, the smoking
lounge with its incomplete jigsaw puzzles,

The great doors clanking behind, and the great
furnaces spewing heat that went right out the windows
you had to open or suffocate; one night she got up
from her bed in the dormitory where she slept with fifty
other women and went to the window and looked out
on deep snow that had fallen the day before
and began to know
what it was she needed.

She needed to be alone, and she needed to come back here.
And so she cast it off, that life she had lived with Ross.

All of it except for the children,

She moved back to Spring Street. On Spring Street was something
she needed. And though there were all kinds of difficulties
with money, with schools, with Ross, who actually wept
about her leaving, out of it she rose, somehow,
altered and alive.

Of course rents had gone up, because of all the new electronics firms on
Route 128, and the apartment came to be too expensive; but during that
year, she became friendly again with the Mexicans and Colombians and
Mrs. Osorio told her about Mr. Jones and his work, and she came here to
the Community Service Center and asked for a child to tutor, and they
gave her Nelson. Nelson Adrian Márquez, who told her right away that he
couldn't read, and then fell, three times in succession, out of his chair.

And it was true enough, she found. He could not read a single word, though
nearly eleven years
old and in fourth grade. How did he get there? And now, today, he still can't
read, in spite of all her efforts…well maybe three words…

She walks down to the tutoring room, past the playroom filled with broken
toys, the two offices: one for the Dots—Savard and Arsenault (no relation
to Alcide) the   other for Mr. Jones. The tutoring rooms are bare with
blackened walls.

As if a fire burned throughout these buildings.
Does it purify, this smoldering?

Nelson is in trouble again. He's been suspended from school, has thrown a
rock through a window of St. Charles. And Mr. Jones has just handed her
the following citation:

…*YEAR OF OUR LORD NINETEEN HUNDRED EIGHTY ONE,
AFORESAID NELSON MARQUEZ, RESIDENT OF ONE HUNDRED
BRANCH STREET, DID REMOVE FROM THE POSSESSION OF ONE
AMANDA AUCOIN THE SUM OF SIXTY CENTS, A BAG OF FRITOS*

AND A PLASTIC PIG...

She has to laugh.

Placing her hand on his chair so he won't tip it, she introduces him again to the long sounds of vowels and how the silent 'e', but he's not having any today, needs a cigarette, and so they sit in clouds of smoke and sound out the syllables he already knows. He's eleven years old, she thinks, almost twelve. There isn't any time before he needs to get a job, to drive a car...

Pat, he reads.
No, Tap.

Sometimes he sees the letters backwards, and sometimes the whole word. He pushes the book away and spills the contents of her pocketbook. Hey, what's this?

A charge card.
This?
A picture of my mother.

He removes the faded photo that's been under a pile of appointment cards. Her mother, who on reaching the age of fifty, and feeling her body failing her, moved out of it. It had come to Priscilla one autumn day as she watched her, posing on the lawn for Harry's camera, this idea that Rika'd vacated her body, found a new enclosure for her soul in the house she had Harry building for her... There it is behind her, almost complete. A house is almost immortal when you compare it to a body. The photo was from a roll of film begun at Luna Lake, where she and Ross had gone to accompany her parents. Harry thought he'd have her nightly on the lumpy double bed in the rustic cabin. He'd another think coming, man of his age, Rika said. She's smiling in the photo, thinking how she'll do the bath in a celery shade...strain of her insomnia about the eyes—Priscilla's inheritance—kept at bay by bicycles, by mixing up her life with people like Megan and Antonia, and Nelson. Hey! he shouts. Dyslexia. She's read a couple books. It's not related, generally, to intelligence. His black eyes snap at her. He speaks two languages. There's speculation that it might be caused by birth anoxia; this disputed by... Hey! ...a claim that it's inherited from the father, linked to left-handedness…caused by a confusion of the two hemispheres. He's right-handed in any case. In any case, untreated, leads to antisocial…other pathology…

Hey! His face is in hers. What's the matter with you?

Thinking, thinking. She puts the pictures, cards away…one of them's gone into his pocket…

You don't need it.

Give it! she shouts.

He hands it to her. He was only fooling.

Listen, I'll read to you awhile.

OK. He sits still a minute while she reads him from a social studies text.

General Knowledge, she calls this part of the lesson. He hasn't any idea what date it is, what time it is, where in the world he is… Someone should have been reading to him all these years, told him things. She shows him a map. See, here's Boston; here's the Charles River… But he's across the room.

Your bike's bein' stole. She's fallen for this one too many times to move. No, come and see the map. He won't.

Untreated leads to antisocial…

It's really bein' stole this time.

She keeps her seat. Look here, I'll show you Puerto Rico.

That little spot? He looks. His father lives there. Not a bad man, really, says *doña* Ramona, his mother; but he drinks.

It's an island, yes; and this is the Atlantic Ocean.

She doesn't know enough, these disabilities…and breaking out in pimples, too. His penis gets *emocionado* he tells her, every time Carmen comes into the room. No, she doesn't know enough.

Pot, reads Nelson.

No, it's top.

Jaysus, Mother Mary, help me," Adie cries, who's messed her pants.

Priscilla goes with Nelson for an airing—they both need it. The sun makes a brief appearance as they're crossing the bridge at Elm, and dances on her river. Nelson, far ahead, is into mud on the bank. He swims here, he tells her, in the summer. He's the only one she knows who possesses the city in the same way she…He's into a car wash now; it has a DO NOT ENTER sign. Of course he cannot read it. He emerges, grinning. Now he finds a dollar in the gutter. There's a hot dog vendor on the corner, and he wants. She buys them each one. They're delicious, and she thinks she probably needs more protein—she's a vegetarian, but neglects to eat sometimes the substitutes, the beans the nuts, and turns like now into a ravening carnivore.

Helen Schade has parked the kitty on the sidewalk in front of Wallex Drug, gone in to buy a *News Tribune,* see if her name is in it from the car that hit her crossing, last week, in front of Grover Cronin's. Yes, it's on the second page:

Helen Sheed (They've spelled her name wrong) a resident of Myrtle Street, was taken via cruiser…treated for abrasions and…

She pushes on across the Chester Brook,

…There was a grist mill here owned by one Thomas Rider; it passed into hands of David Mead and his descendants in the latter part of the Eighteenth Century, and under Moses Mead, became a factory which manufactured wooden handles used for axes, hayrakes, pestles, rolling pins and such.

And to the foot of Piety Corner…

So named because the deacons of First Parish Church once occupied its substantial houses…

The garage sale is a disappointment. Some dirty placemats and Christmas ornaments, a rusty meat grinder. She has her pride; but buys a plastic pocketbook and a plaster Stella Maris, so as not to have walked so far for nothing.

Coming back, she spots
A squirrel without a tail.
Third sign today
she'll meet a stranger.

Last night she dreamed of a lion (at the gate?)

No, it was a tiger. Just before she woke. She
threw it a child to keep it off, then, in remorse
for what she'd done, herself.

Ickle puddy sleeping on the blankets. She gets a key to the restroom at
Colwin's. Dirty. She takes a napking from her cart and wipes out the sink.

I Dreamt I Dwelt in Marble Halls, hums Megan, on commode.
There's something wrong with this Margo. She seems to have locked herself
in the bathroom. Megan thinks she's preggers.

Back at the Service Center, Nelson swipes Priscilla's bike and starts to take
off. She grabs it by the seat and dumps him off. You do that and I call the
cops, she hollers at him, and he walks right away from her. She goes and
grabs him, pulls him to her.
Listen. I didn't mean to say that word. Calmer now, she holds him by both
arms. It's not a thing a friend does, is it?
    No. He shakes his head.
    And I'm your friend, and so I won't; but listen, though, it doesn't mean
I won't call someone, she goes on.
    Call who?
    Well, someone like Antonia's husband, she's inspired to say. He's a big
man, strong, in spite of being sick. A stern father…comes to help paint the
offices, sometimes, carry out the trash, Jesús Roldán. The only father about
this place.

Nelson's nodding. Yeah, he says, OK, impressed. He gets her bike and she
locks it up, feeling weary. They go in and she makes him work awhile on
the lamp they're making out of wood scraps—knobs and discs and spindle
shapes they got at a warehouse down on Water Street. The electric parts
they got at Woolworth's. She sets the paints before him: magenta, ochre,
rose. They'll try to sell this one at the fair next month, she's thinking; he'll
get money, learn that stealing's not the only…What's it matter he can't
read? He'll work, she thinks. Yes, in a simpler age he'd be apprenticed to
a carpenter, a fatherly shoemaker…In spite of recent disappointments
concerning Mao and his revolution, she'd once been so ardent about after
that production of Fanshen in Boston she'd gone to with David while she

was still a student at Mount Holyoke, she clung to notions of what…? Of a society unlike this one she lived in…Poorer, more attuned to need, not desire. Must it always end up like this, this Gang of Four?

Hey!

What?

You doin' it again.

Thinking, yes… I was thinking about the little boys in Iran. That make the beautiful rugs.

What beautiful rugs?

Persian rugs, they're called. Little boys have been making them for centuries. I used to have one in my house.

And how they make them.

They make little silk knots in different beautiful colors, to form designs that their great great great grandfathers made up from looking at nature. They are something like puzzles. And these designs were passed down from father to son, or mother to son. I'm not sure.

There were so many things she wasn't sure of, she only half knew. So much she read about or forgot, or couldn't connect to anything else. And now there was no time to remedy this.

They have to do it? He asks.

Do what?

Make the knots?

Yes, that's the bad thing. They have to work many hours a day all week, and they can't go to school.

They don't have to go to school? he says hopefully.

They can't. They have to earn money for their families to eat. They would like to go to school.

No, they wouldn't.

Yes, they really would. If they were to go to school, they could earn more money; but I think, in a way, they must be happy as they are.

Nelson paints his fingernails magenta. She retrieves the magenta.

I'll help you. She picks up a brush. Is this your brush or mine?

It's yours! he shouts. It's *all* yours, don't you know

Of course it's hers, the lamp, the whole construction in her head. She'd like to give it to him, but she can't. Untreated leads to…

And yet, she tells herself, she sometimes gets it right. I won't call them, police, but I'll call someone. Yes, she got that right.

Eulalie rests in a broth of sunlight on a bench in front of the Banks Square House. In front of her Arizona Johnson, a little girl from the project, sits on the curb and puts on her roller skates. Her little brother, Painter Johnson, stands on an old tire watching her with his stomach stuck out. A man with headphones on is passing a metal detector over the scruffy lawn. He stoops, picks up a rusted nut.

Eulalie wonders what could possibly be the benefits of this apparatus. Coins, someone told her once. They look for coins and diamond rings that someone's lost. But how many coins would you have to pick up to even pay for the machine. And what are your chances, really, of finding someone's wedding ring or such…?

It's only five, but Henrietta Rose, instead of going home first, has walked up to the Waltham Spa and had tea and a muffin, lingering over it an hour, and thence to the basement of St. Charles, known as the Italian Church, where she starts the coffee for the meeting at seven. A humble coffeemaker after ten years sober. One doesn't get above oneself; she's learned that lesson. It's difficult with two canes, and John the Indian is usually here to help, or else Dave, that shy new boy that rides a bicycle; but it's too early for John and these shy new boys on bicycles because they've lost their licenses until well into the next century are given to lapses. She puts on the hissing pot and digs out the powdered creamer and the lumpy sugar from the steamer trunk on the floor behind the stage, moving slowly with one cane. She'll see tonight if she can do it all herself. From a tilting file cabinet, she takes the photo of Bill Wilson stuck among the plaster madonnas and the catechism workbooks—Seven Bulwarks of a Catholic Home. There's a votive candle in here somewhere—they light it for the still-suffering alcoholics, and a framed needlepoint of the Steps. She sets the speaker's table up like a little altar. A few people come in. The homeless and semi homeless deposit themselves in corners like the victims of a bomb: a young man with his foot in plaster, a young girl weeping over supper in a paper sack. She asks the young man with the foot to set up the literature rack. The lame and the halt, she thinks, but it is done.

The coffee's done. She takes some, creams it with some ghastly stuff, and pokes in the messy trunk to find some oatmeal raisin cookies, sets them out. Still a half an hour until starting time.

The child of the weeping girl is on the floor with crayons and a coloring book. He's about the age of hers when she was drinking *Bwana Bap*, The People's Drink It's funny that she can't recall her children in that setting. Husband, yes, herself, atop an elephant... When did they menstruate? When sprout pubic hair?

Priscilla locks her bike to the swing set and climbs. The elevator hasn't worked for several months, and there's a pervasive smell of rotting mop.

Frostie' s home, standing in front of the open refrigerator. She fixes tea.

Find what you want and close, she says to Frostie. You think I'm made of money? Where are the others? she asks.

He tells her Solie took Benno to the store, and says, There isn't any juice. There isn't any anything.

There's last night's casserole we're going to have soon as I rest a minute, she says.

He shuts the door and walks around the table eating a slice of bread.

Ma, I...

Stop milling.

I'm not milling. Ma I need your signature is all, and six dollars...

Six dollars! I might have thirty cents, you hunt through all my pockets...

...to rent the skis...

The skis!

All the other kids have their own, of course.

In Varnum Circle, kids have skis?

Well it's the school that's going, not the project. Can't you write a...

A check! Rent skis! What do you need the skis for? To come down a mountain, right? Now if we lived on top of a mountain, there would be some sense; but since we live in Varnum Circle, Waltham, Massachusetts, where there isn't even snow this time of...

Ma!

They must transport you to this mountain…
Ma, the bus is free. The school pays!

Pay attention to them…
Who said that to her?
Oh, that woman at the Sunshine Club. Who played the harp.
But first she must finish this:
So they must transport you to this mountain, and then up the mountain, where you must rent skis to come down it!
Ma!
Usually he'd follow her in this.
And someone, somewhere has to pay for it. Nothing's free, speaks the great granddaughter of Enoch Rowan, a socialist since she's seventeen.
Oh, here, she says, taking up her bag and finding her last ten. And get a hamburger if you want.
 You see my logic, though?
Yeah. But going down is worth it.
Hah. You are my wonderful boy. And I should appreciate you more.
 Thanks, Ma, thanks!
How can there be snow? It's April.
Oh, there's snow. Or they make it.
Make it! And what can that cost!

She shakes herself and takes her teacup to the sink. She can't be battling everything all the time.
She used to like the notion of going very fast over snow herself. But the snow was never manufactured.

This crosscountry skiing must be nice. Why can't you do that?
Maybe when I'm old as you.
Ah, yes. Did Solie do her homework?
I don't think so. I did mine.

Solie.

She was first.
The first child comes and colonizes,
fells the trees to make that first clearing,
where the others come and settle comfortably,
alert and curious, like Frostie; and
babyish and playful like Benno;
But never vigilant for tigers like the first.

What did Solie pick up when she was sleeping in that bureau drawer
on Spring Street? That her mother worried about the world ending
in nuclear disaster? There must have been something communicated
to her by the boxes stored everywhere with provisions, by the night
alarms, the hastily called meetings, the arguments between David and
Ross, between David and herself. The house in Weston must have
seemed to keep off the tigers. She worried about the world, like her
mother; but not in the same way.

While Young and Crippen Sleep

Aboard Columbia Young and Crippen sleep

It was a trying afternoon, I must say, Megan says to Margo, whose face has all come out in blotches.. And no one enjoyed it. Except for the music. And I'm sure I was the only one that listened. Priscilla tried to get me something decent from the Bookmobile. I wanted something on Elizabeth the First, and all they have is this present Elizabeth. World's most boring woman. All she cares about are dogs and horses. Ought to let her son reign. At least, they say, he has some other interests... The girl isn't hearing a word she says. And she's only babbling on so that the poor creature can get a hold on herself, so there isn't a scene.

John The Indian arrives and sets up the sound system at the basement of St. Charles. Young Ronnie chairs the meeting, and asks the young man with the foot to read 'How it Works' out of the Big Book. Never heard of periods or commas, seems. All the results of our shoddy education system on display here. But Henrietta admires them for taking on this difficult literature. Bill Wilson liked big words and long sentences. Any other organization she ever knew would have long ago modernized all this, taken out the references to the Depression, the iron lungs and all; and put in gender neutral pronouns, of course, even the Congregationalists have that...But we've more important things to...and it heartens her to see these, scruffy, half educated young men learn to read sitting around a table and reading the Big Book and the Step Book over and over like primers. For you never finished with them. You started over. Salutary for a high speed reader of novels like herself. Once, in her step group, she met a newcomer, a rather elegant woman like herself, who graduated from Radcliffe. They finished up step twelve that night, and, she remembers, the woman asked her what they would read next. We go back to step one, Henrietta told her. My God, how boring, said the woman and she never came back.

Winnie, at the window in her nighty, notes the horse and rider caught in the branches of the beech tree opposite, points it out to Margo.

Rearing, can't you see it?
Margo can't

How do you think it got there? Winnie asks.

Oh, Winnie, please...

Adie gabbles up the pap that Margo's mashed her. Nothing spoils Adie's appetite except a birthday party, and now that's forgotten except for two paper napkins and a cardboard cover to a coffee cup, a plaster rose off her cake she's hidden beneath the cushion of her chair. Why can't... Margo is thinking she won't make it till eleven. Why can't they...? He either climbs or flies, says Winnie. My guess is that he flies; and still I never catch...

Helen Schade is heating up a cup of chocolate. The cat weaves among the objects on her table without disturbing any of them, sits and stares at her with his yellow eyes. Came back to me did you, ingrate. Yes, a lowlife cat you whoring after Tender Vittles come back begging Missy Helen for your blanky spanky shall I spank you? what you're asking for? I've half a mind to eat myself sardines I bought you. I like them too myself you're not the only...puddentane look at him making his nest there in behind by sugar pot, hiding self ashamed for shame then pull your tail in then and curl it round you lowlife cat come back to Missy Helen shameless. Hide himself he better or I'll noggin him, he had his little adventure did he tired of his Missy is he? Ingrate. He thinks he'll chase that half-wit with his hands in his pants the dirty luring kitties with his Tender Vittles. Evil, don't you know he's thinking evil thinking later he may strangle one and hide the body in the ash bin happens all the time and he'd be sorry then, my gentleman, no running back to Missy and his blanky hear me do you? Yes I see his tail twitch he understands me every word the poppet. Yes, he understands me every word the puddentane the poppet I'll poppet him I will his Missy doesn't like ingratitude she oughter leave him to his half-wit leave him lock her door I see his little ear there twitching he wouldn't leave his Missy Helen would he? Clean his tail there all around his little shit hole pink his pinky tongue and pinky pads and little pinky shit hole, cute he walks about and shows it off his tail up shameless as a lowlife hussy, Missy ought to noggin him yes clean yourself make yourself all pretty shiny black for Missy so she'll take you back yes take you back with all your little special little special...lets you in her bed and on her table with your little dish your pwiveleges a pwivileged puss you Missy's wittle gentleman in little formal wear all black and white and with a wittle mustache lick it yes and wash the half-wit off you dirty half-wit with his hands inside his pants he's out to catch a kitty taken in by treats and lock him somewhere where he can't get back to Missy ever yes and he'll be sorry, he'll be sorry, no more rides in Missy's cart and no more sips of Missy's coffee creamers… yawning look at him he doesn't mind his Missy ought to make him walk back, have to scratch at the door like other cats he's sorry yes he's sorry now the ickle…

Margo's back with Adie in the bedroom…Who was it, Megan calls out, wrote that book on Mozart?
She was the daughter of the singer Alma Gluck. Oh, well, you wouldn't know; you're far too young.

There's something owed the young, too, Margo thinks.
Why don't they die?
Lovey Mother, Adie yells

What *was* her name? Megan asks herself. It was the same, she's thinking, as some town in Iowa…Davenport! Yes, Marcia Davenport! Megan says out loud, but Margo's in the bathroom crying. Adies's hit her; didn't want her corset off.

Margo tells herself that Adie doesn't under…just it hurt her, catching the earpiece of her glasses, causing them to dig into her nose. She's overwrought, is all. It's no use blaming them.

It wasn't them that got you pregnant. Of course not. It's she, herself, that's thrown away her education, simply. She can't possibly go back until this baby's out of diapers, and then her credits will be useless.

Marcia Davenport was Alma Gluck's mother, says Megan, marveling at her brain's capacities.

Two gentlemen of leisure, the Professor, badly listing, and the kid they call the Maggot, have taken themselves to dine at St. Charles Borromeo where the ladies of the Altar Guild are serving beans and franks. The Professor chooses two pairs of trousers from the clothes box and holds them up. Which of these, har, do you think the better? He rolls his dirty eyeballs at Mary Regan, ladling beans.

Have to do an essay, Frostie tells his mother, about who I think's the greatest man our age.

Hmm, Priscilla takes this up while getting out the casserole and sprinkling some extra cheese. Churchill, Charles de Gaulle? Chairman Mao…

You want to catch a pair of hummingbirds in coitus you need a slow motion camera, Megan tells Margo, who has almost thrown her dinner at her. On the other hand, with frogs, the sexual embrace can last for weeks.

Eulalie relaxes in her bath. Alcide fed, in bed with rails up, teeth in the container. Helen Schade is coming in to watch him while she goes to choir practice. She lifts a fine-boned ankle and admires her silky calf. No hint of veins.

She remembers baths in the farmhouse kitchen
The blackened copper tub, her sisters plaiting
their hair in the steamy room and pressing their ruffled
dresses with the tall black iron that you filled with stove coals…

Oh, the farm was happiness. But there
were too many of them.
Not all could stay. She and her sister Helene
must come here to work.

How they wept that first winter on Cherry Street.
Walking the block to work in the dark, and home again
in darkness, to wash their stockings, dry them on
the sill. Their hearts back on the farm,

The steaming kitchen, saving up their pay
so they could return.
Hoping always they'd be asked to stay,

But never were. For here was work, The Mill,
Le Watch. She cleaned the undersides
of looms, then kept the spindles loaded, bettering
herself; .she walked demure down Moody Street,

Eyes on her lace up boots,
and the young men's eyes on her.

Eulalie! A voice in the steamy bath.
Who calls?
Your bust!
Who? What?

Examine your bust, Eulalie!

Dieu, who speaks! Above her right nipple, she finds it…size of a grape…
heartstopped in the perspiring lilac tile bath, she tastes corruption.
Sacre! Yes, it's there. No doubt. Her mother's voice, she recognized it.
Her lump found when she was fifty; killed her six years later. She recalls
the grotesque, swollen arm. They cut it off to spare her the inert weight.
A dead thing, it preceded her to the grave. Giddy with quick breathing,
she sits on the hopper, throws her wrapper over her. Through the fabric
she can't feel it.

The two largest brains in history were Aknaton and Sir Isaac Newton,
Megan tells Margo. Newton's brain is preserved in vinegar somewhere.

The agency calls Margo back.
I can't, I can't another minute. I'm sick. I'm going to kill someone!
They're going to send Priscilla, they tell her.

She's shaking all over as she puts the pills in paper cups: Elavil to elevate,
and Mellaril to ameliorate, and Restoril to restorate. She always studies
the literature that comes with them from the pharmacy: Reduced
libido, lowered sperm…laboratory trials show a count reduced to forty
million sperm per cubic…
Well, it's only one you need, she thinks.

Priscilla dozing when they call her in. Frostie and his sister Solie gone up to the roof with Frostie's telescope. She'll come, yes, till Rosa gets there at eleven, she tells them, but give her twenty minutes. She clears the table and eats the bread crescents left on the plates. Benno comes and winds himself around her. To bed. You must. Mummy must go out again.

No!

Only for a couple hours. Solie's here. Solie is his mother. Fierce and vigilant for tigers. Benno has interesting nightmares and always it is Solie who takes him in her bed.

I might dream about the raccoon again.
But raccoons are gentle animals. They are vegetarians.
What's vegetarian?
They eat carrots and tomatoes. They steal from gardens. It's their only offense.
What's offense?
Crime. Well not crime. We are the criminals. We take all the space away from them, to grow our
own vegetables.
And put a fence. That's why it's called offense, he says.
Well, maybe there's a connection.
The raccoon in my dream has pointed teeth. I shine my flashlight at him and he has pointed teeth.
That's something you remember from when we lived with Daddy. We heard a noise one night and Daddy went out with his flashlight to see and surprised some raccoons in the trash.
Well, when I tell Solie the dream, she's afraid with me. And Daddy was afraid.
No, he was just finding out what was the matter, and putting the lids on tight. When you think of a raccoon, just think he's hungry and wants to get your old peanut butter sandwich crusts…
And one was sick once.
Oh, yes, I remember. They came out of the Welfare once, when Benno was quite small, and there was a raccoon sitting on the stoop. He looked sick.

That was much more scary than the raccoon in the trash. I didn't want you to touch him because he might have been sick.
And you went back in to get a piece of bread.
Oh, yes. She'd thought he either must be sick or hungry to be just sitting there on the stoop like one of the Welfare recipients.
Maybe he was just hungry, she says. Did he eat the bread, do you remember?
I think he did.

I hope so. Sick scares me, but pointed teeth don't. We have two pointed teeth. She points to her cuspids.
Come to bed now. She gathers up his bones, his elbow in her collarbone as he fingers his cuspids. Then puts her uniform back on and goes up to call Solie down.
Who's that? she asks about the shadowy figure with Frostie.
That's Nelson Márquez.
If he gets caught, he'll go to jail. It's past the curfew. Ah, well. She can't make everything right.

Nelson Márquez, you go home! she shouts, nevertheless, into the darkness. And to her daughter Soledad she says with even less hope: You'll do your homework please. I have to work a couple hours.

O.K.

She might and she might not, Priscilla thinks. She's failing math and science. Her English and history grades are good however.
And she will make sure that Benno's O.K. That's all she can count on. People do what they want, she tells herself and tries to remember it's how she operates herself.

They won't cut her, not this body, Eulalie tells herself, and takes heart from this resolve, standing before the foggy mirror and repeating,
Pas!

There's a potluck supper at the Baptist Church on Lexington Street. A talk and slide show on El Salvador. The Reverend Thomas Withbroe. The

Professor dozes comfortably through it.

Helen Schade is come while Eulalie finishes dressing. She puts on the TV and seats herself before it. Eulalie, carrying corruption, comes in and says goodbye to Helen. She's put the urinal beside Alcide, will be back by ten, she tells her.

No hurry, says Helen comfortably.

The Professor snores softly in the slideshow dark.

Ramona Márquez drags her son home, locks him up, and goes to services at La Iglesia de Cristo Misionera in the chapel of the Congregational Church. The minute that she's gone, he's out the bathroom window to the roof of Building B, where Frostie's left the door propped open.

Priscilla mounts her bike and coasts the block to Norumbega. Martin Luther King, she's thinking, was he the greatest man our age...? But there were those before him, Dorothy Day, Thoreau... Well that was another century... A streetlight's out in front of the Welfare, makes a sinister scene from out of some old black and white movie. She skirts the the Common with its warm lights and reassuring bus passengers at the south end, and goes straight up Moody without her morning detour over the little footbridge by the Mill. She's late, but thinks she'll need some coffee to get through this shift and locks her bike to the stop sign outside the Waltham Spa and goes in to fill her thermos.

Eulalie's there, buying her fourth of a ticket for the lottery.

Did Alcide come back? Priscilla asks. He come back with police, Eulalie says, I hide his walker and then he go out again. He is impossible.

Yes, impossible. She wonders what accounts for deadness in Eulalie's voice—usually she would cry, imposs ee ble on a rising note.

Are you all right? Priscilla asks.

Eulalie turns her long and complicated French face with its elongated ears and jowls and its slight tremor toward Priscilla, and there's no seeing into it.

Of course, there is nothing the matter. He is home with Helen Schade now and the rails up...

If that's any guarantee of anything, Priscilla thinks. Eulalie appears to have lost her sense of fun.

She sips some of her coffee, then puts it into her backpack and gets her bike and rides on, using the sidewalk here, though it's forbidden for bicycles. It was on this block, just past the Irish Travel Bureau, a car came down Myrtle Street and sideswiped her, throwing her into a hedge. The incident replays itself with variations on eighteen wheelers; fortuitous hedges replaced by concrete or fences with iron spikes. She shakes the scenes out of her head, pedaling vigorously up Adams Street.

Just a warning to her to be careful, that incident. She is more careful now than in those days of scaling fences and lying down in front of massed policemen with truncheons. She was never afraid then, never imagined real danger. Still can't. It was all a drama, with a foregone conclusion... It was all in the cause of peace and...

Gandhi! she thinks. Gandhi, of course! How could she not think of it? Gandhi was the greatest man of our age.

She locks her bike to the iron railing. Margo's got the door open and her jacket on. You sick? Priscilla asks.

Yes, sick, I can't...

Well, wait a minute.

No, I have to get out of here, Margo cries, and she's off down the street without giving report even. Oh well, she'll get it another day, or make it up. None of them are above making up a report: quiet night, you wrote, changed bed once. Or: restless night, changed bed three times...

But what could be wrong with everyone tonight?

She's preggers, Megan tells her. I can always tell. Megan is on the couch with *Opera News* and a Public Television offering on. Her eyes are bright with mischief, and Priscilla sees a hint of victory over Margo in them. She avoids her for the time to tend to Adie, who has messed herself, and the laundry which is piling up. She puts the load she finds in washer into dryer, loads the washer with what's in the basket and puts Adie's sheets to soak. Yes, Gandhi, she thinks. She wishes she could tell Frostie. When she gets a minute, she'll call. Then she gets Winnie up and strongarms her on to the toilet. Megan's watching the news. It seems the would-be assassin of the President is the son of a wealthy Texas oil man. His apparent motive was to win the affection of a teen-aged movie actress that he's never met. My

aotronomer is on next, Megan tells her. We'll watch it together.
    OK, Priscilla says, walking Winnie back to bed.

Eulalia, carrying her new knowledge, crosses
Spring Street, notes the green car pulled up at
the circle: Leo Blakey, that Megan's brother.
Good brother, that one, she thinks. He never married.
Had his sister Winnie home with him
until she took her stroke.

Funny, thinks Eulalie, how your life
goes on, your thoughts go on in spite of…
She hopes that Helen Shade
will be all right with Alcide.
She still hears voices sometimes.

Nelson Márquez, child of criminal tendency,
encounters Frostie on the roof, pulls out
his stash of stolen watches hiddenin a
hollow concrete block and passes one of them to Frostie.

La Schade has checked Eulalie's fridge and eaten
two greenolives. She's hearing voices telling
her to steal some writing paper,
write her sister Maddie,
tell her some home truths…

Frostie studies the cheap digital watch.
They're stole from Woolworths, Nelson says.
Me and Dennis gonna move one.
Frostie's figuring the economics:

A coolie in Taiwan made maybe, twenty cents
its manufacture. Woolworth's buys it wholesale lots.
They're of course, the losers when a kid like
Nelson takes it off their hands.

We get the money, we pay Ana for a
fucking lesson, Nelson says to Frostie.
The establishment, in short, is robbed
the value of one fuck, thinks Frostie, who's
his mother's son.

A kind of justice, yes…
He focuses his telescope on Sirius
in the Greater Dog. He cannot see
its dark companion.

    Listen, Nelson, you think Dennis can?
    I mean has he arrived at puberty? He asks.
    At where?
    Has he got hair, I mean,
    down there?

Frostie, you are mad, his sister Solie says.
I got, Nelson says. You want to see?
Not really.
You got?
No, says Frostie.

    I'm on the slow side.
    The median age is twelve.
    And she, you sister?
    Solie, you got hair? Kid wants to know.

Hair where?
Oh well, we know you got it on your head.

Leo Blakey comes up the steps to visit his sisters. He goes in to Winnie first.
My name is Winnie Blakey and I live at number twenty Aspenwall, says
Winnie by way of introduction.
I know that, says her brother, aware that thirty years ago they lived at
twenty Aspenwall.
    And who are you?

Your brother Leo, Winnie.

Well I'm pleased to know you. I've been talking in my sleep they tell me.

Have you? So do I sometimes.

They're giving me a pill, the doctors. Do they give you too?

For talking in my sleep? Oh, no, I just don't tell them.

They don't like me doing it. I wake them up and make them jump. Say, what's your name again?

I'm Leo, Winnie. Leo Blakey.

Well, I'm sure it's very nice to meet you. Listen, there's another thing. I don't tell anyone...

What is it, Sissy?

There's a lion in the tree out front. A *couchant* lion.

Is there now?

Couchant, rampant.

You don't tell them though. It's wiser not.

Oh, absolutely. There'd be trouble. What's your name again? You're very kind.

It's Leo, Winnie.

You want to see my armpits? Solie offers, then goes down to watch her brother Benno, having exacted a promise from Frostie to spell her later, so she can go to Nelson's apartment.

What do you think, says Megan to Priscilla, this fuss about the presidential health? Now, Grover Cleveland had a cancer of the lip you know. He smoked a pipe. They operated on him out at sea in a hospital ship. The public didn't need to know the gristly details. Yet one does, want to know. At least in the case of someone interesting. Most of them, including this present incumbent, aren't of much interest. I've heard enough already. Was it you told me this afternoon I should try fiction?

I think so. I mean there isn't much else on the Bookmobile...

No, no! I've no time for fiction. Facts are what I need...

'Old men ought to be explorers,' quotes Priscilla.

Who said that?

I think it was Eliot. Thomas Stearnes.

And did he say old women too? asks Megan.

Henrietta, leaning on her canes, awaits the bus from Roberts, sees it stop a block ahead of stop, and wonders will he pass her, runs out to wave.

Madame, you run in front of me…I might have…

Chance I had to take. You pass me by, I have to wait another hour. And you stopped before

the stop, she informs him. A bus is supposed to stop at stops!

Fumbling in her pocketbook for fare, she notes that he's an Indian—bruised skin about the eyes, the loopy forelock. Yes, an Indian would ibe vague about the stops. She sits, a little sorry—always had a soft spot for them—thinks she'll ask his pardon later. Let him stew a little first and learn to keep his wits about…

You ever wonder, Megan says, to Priscilla, how birds copulate?

Alcide wakes and sneezes, gets up and rummages in drawers. Involved in her letter, Helen Schade doesn't hear him.

And there's a traffic jam near Bemis. Henrietta's Indian has taken up a little reedy flute, is tootling one of those tiresome melodies that she remembers. Yes, he must calm himself, she thinks. An Indian must always calm himself. It's odd. She never knew one drive a bus—except, incompetently, in their own country. They weren't cut out for it. This one is most likely a dreamy astrophysics student nights, or some such pursuit.

The traffic is moving slowly past the old Murphy General Hospital—now housing overflow from the National Archives: papers of the Continental Congress, Indian Treaties, histories of the coastal forts and lighthouses, Daniel Webster's papers, tax returns, patents on Paul Moody's power loom, genealogies… Yes, the Montague's traced their ancestry to William Brewster; there were some other clergymen of note, but a surprising number of them came to no good end; one of her great uncles spend his prime in jail… She wonders if William Brewster was an alcoholic…

There is stir among the passengers. She looks out the window at an unfamiliar lighted square.

Where is she going? She takes out her memo pad and asks her seatmate what day it is.

Tuesday, he says.

And this is supposedly a Bemis bus…

Yes a Bemis bus. She always takes it home after the meeting at St. Charles Borromeo; but it seems to be taking a different route. I get off at Walnut, she says to the man.

Well, we're nowhere near Walnut.

Pardon me, but is this a Bemis bus? a woman at the back calls out to the driver.

No, I am Kenmore, says the driver pleasantly. He has put his flute away and has found an open road, which he is plunging down with a bit of abandon which seems unwarranted. Kenmore. We're going to

Kenmore. We just passed Lewando's Laundry, mutters the man beside Henrietta, and suddenly everyone is shouting at once:

Bemis. It says Bemis on your sign! Just look! God, we're miles out of…this is crazy…

The woman from the back has gone forward and is trying to correct his course, while he protests that he has always been a Kenmore bus, and reaches up to twirl the dial of his sign.

No, you are Bemis! shouts the woman. We are all Bemis passengers, and now we will all be late. It has already happened, sighs the man next to Henrietta, looking at his watch. He must stay calm, thinks Henrietta. We must stay calm.

But no one is calm. The shouting woman finally convinces him to turn, so that they are bumping over streets that no bus ever took, with the woman browbeating him at every corner: turn here! Turn here! fuming through long red lights and bumping over curbs. And now cars are honking at them. We're way into Watertown, says the man next to Henrietta. A car is honking in the other lane, just below their window. The man opens it, and they hear some words that sound like…hijacked! Are we hijacked? No, no, Henrietta's seatmate shouts out the window. Just an idiot. But he isn't heard. The bus comes to a sudden stop, throwing the instruction-giving woman into the driver's lap. Two police cruisers have parked in front of them. The officers burst in and drag the driver out of his seat and onto the pavement.

But he must have calm, thinks Henrietta. And I was going to apologize to him. Meanwhile her seat mate has been forward and has obtained some information. He comes back and explains: The headboard…He must have

turned it to HELP when he was fooling with it. We've been driving all over
two towns on a bus that says HELP.

    Well, we needed help, didn't we? says Henrietta reasonably. You know
I lived in India. They are an extraordinary people. They have a great deal of
intelligence and talent, but some of them should not drive buses.

Alcide wakes and sneezes. Marry her…thinks Alcide. It's the only answer.
He's out of bed and rummaging in drawers. Achoo!
But Helen Schade doesn't hear it.

She's hearing voices speaking French or something,
like those nurses at the State.
Haitians.

They were mostly Haitians. Had last names
that sounded like first names: L'Eveque Nancy
was the woman who escorted them to therapy,
jingling her keys and opening the heavy
doors that crashed behind.

She was nice. She gave them hugs. They called
her Nannie Lecky, trotting after her
in their shoes without the laces. Why couldn't
they have laces? O, there was that kid
who tried to hang himself by his…

And she was careful with us. Used to check us
every fifteen minutes, even in the bath:
You in dere, Helen, Honey?
Yeah, I'm digging out the grunge under my
big toe with a plastic fork, she'd holler out.
Impossible to croak yourself with a plastic fork.
She knew because she'd tried.
She tickled Helen, Nannie Lecky. She'd run back to her
if she could. To Nannie Lecky…

You in dere, Helen?

Yes, I'm taking off my purple stockings,
washing them in the basin. Now I'm looking
at my pores in Eulalie's magnifying mirror.
I have some things in my pocketbook you wouldn't like.

A lady's razor, all my pills. If you
could see me now you'd come and grab me.

You weren't like the social workers with their contracts:
you sign here and you can see your sister for a weekend.
You just grabbed us, held us to your bosom.

Helen, what you doing now? says voice of Nanny Lecky in her head. I'm watering this yellow plant Eulalie has that can't decide to live or die. Plant reminds her of those two old desiccated senior citizens on Lura Lane, her parents. If they would die, she could live comfortable in a twelve room house.

Or if the other voices, not these kind ones, did come back, she could afford a private hospital with that nice blond furniture and the snacks in the refrigerator and the fruit bowls on the tables, and the libraries full of books and stereos, and the puzzles with all the pieces. But the yellow desiccated cast deceives. They're like this plant and will outlive me like the long line of pricks that I'm descended from. Or if they die, she'll get it all, who doesn't need it.

Helen. What you doing Helen? She's found Eulalie's lilac writing pad, has borrowed Eulalie's Parker pen to bring her sister up to date about the last fifteen years of her life

Missed an education, but left the State ten years ago and found myself a little room, she writes. The luxury—a room all to myself instead of that dorm they locked you out of after breakfast until suppertime, the filthy, noisy day room… I entertain myself. Don't think I sit around and wait for you to call. I go to yard sales, and just last week a car ran into me and my name was in the paper…

Only they misspelled my name. Sheed, they spelled it.

Achoo! Alcide sneezes

I read a lot of books, too, spite of never going to college…voices, they took care of that. Just now I'm reading one from the library about a doctor that treats an otter has a spine stuck in his…

I come across a word that I don't know, I look it up in the diction…

Something crashes loudly in the bedroom, but she chooses to ignore it.

…dictionary. 'Ubiquitous'. I bet you don't know what that word means. Everywhere, it means. Everywhere, all the time. Oh, well you probably know it being a college graduate and all…You always were the lucky one. I knew it since that day you got the part I wanted…Emily in Our Town. I always knew

I was a better actress, but you were prettier, and the kids chose you…

Another crash.

Would've been different if the teacher'd chosen— like she should have. Teachers always favored me; they saw my promise. Kids, what do kids know about talent…pick the prettiest, most popular. We put a play on in the hospital. I was a shell-shocked soldier in it. I frightened everyone; I was so good. Your eyes, they said, your eyes were chilling.

Achooo!

Helen Schade has rummaged in another drawer and found a lilac envelope to match the stationery, enclosed and sealed her letter, realizes only then that she's forgotten long ago the number and the street name where her sister lives…

Ach OOO!

She goes, finds Alcide out of bed and barefoot, opening all the drawers and throwing clothes all over the floor.

What do you think you're doing?

Marry her. Give the child a name. The man's the one to take respons… ach ooo!

See there, you've gone and caught a cold. Get back in bed. I'll call Eulalie!

Go ahead. A man's a man! My teeth, my cane. Where are my…

Helen shuts the door on him. He's made her lose her train of thought.

Old men ought to be explorers.' I like that, says Megan. Old women too. What makes them different? Menstruation, it's menstruation makes girls different. Hated it. It's not…how can I put it? Not elegant, like other things in nature. Not economical. And it holds girls back while boys go off adventuring. Degrading if you ask me, too. You had a set of towels, before these sanitary napkins, and you had to hem them up, then wash and iron them. It took a lot of time when you might have been doing something more edifying.

Cleopatra, I remember reading somewhere, used a sachet of crushed roses…

A sachet of crushed roses! Wonderful, exclaims Priscilla. Wherever did you read it?

Oh, I'm a mine of information, Megan says. An autodidact, Louie used to call me, and I never went beyond the tenth grade. Yes, an autodidact. I bet you don't know what country has the highest number of saints per capita…

Priscilla doesn't.

South Korea. South Korea has a saint for every thirteen million people. I read that. Yes, I always was a reader. They used to catch me reading *Anthony Adverse* under the counter in my father's store. 'Dear Heavenly Father, can't the child go out and play?' my Pa would holler. 'Go out and get yourself some air! Dear God, the child's pale as death!' I'd go and toss a ball against the cellar door for fifteen minutes, then come begging to come back. Came by it honestly, in any case. A family affliction.

Words. My Ma would write a three page letter telling Pa to come to supper. Print. We had a love of print; and great reciters, too, of verse. My Uncle Leo used to render D'Arcy's 'Face on the Barroom Floor' at the drop of a… And Irish tenor, Uncle Leo. Funny, isn't it how Russia gives us basses, and Ireland, tenors. You remember Dennis Day? MacMahon was his real name. A brother of his married Ann Blyth. D'Arcy, yes, Antoine D'Arcy wrote that song. I imagine he's forgotten now.

Nelson and Dennis have made a deal with a kid from Thornton Road to sell two watches, split the fourteen dollars. Dennis goes off on his own. Hey, yells Nelson, running to keep up. You ask her can I watch?

    She don't like kids. I tol you.

    You a kid.

    She making an exception. Now you want to make her make two exceptions.

The professor, gentleman loafer and knight of the road,
passes the boys as he weaves toward the trestle.
He notes the gray squirrel, recent victim of
a hesitation, crossing Prospect Street in heavy traffic…
foot raised in final rictus under a streetlamp,
fur still stirring with electric life.

The news of this demise will just this moment
be arriving at the Creator's ear, he thinks.
Becoming part of the sum of ancient knowledge
of a universe that's finitely expanding—

Unlike Megan, the professor's a fitful proponent
of a contracting universe: a seed containing
the whole, in portent or in memory:
the knowledge of this gray squirrel's death and fact
of his—the Professor's—having on
this night in April a bellyful of beans
and franks served by the Ladies of the Holy Name…

Hey, listen, Nelson skips to catch up to Dennis, I'm the one had the idea first, remem…

    OK, OK, says Dennis, climbing the dark stair to Ana's.

    She opens wearing a purple wrapper. Two of them! she screams. *Dos mocosos! No me digas!*

    He just wants to watch us, Dennis tells her, indicating Nelson.

    Watch us?

    And he pay you too. We both pay you.

    Yes, and then his Mama keel me!

But they're through the door already and in the livingroom. Nelson's never seen a room like this, the dove gray velvet sectional, the lamps, the cushions. Dennis starts into the bedroom...

Nelson Márquez, you stay there and don't touch nothing, *oyes*! or I tell your Mama, Ana screams.

Meanwhile, Dennis has his pants and shirt off, is starting on his socks. You got to take the socks off too? says Ana, lolling on the tiger skin that covers the bed. Her purple robe is fallen open to reveal her dusky breasts, and Nelson's penny's getting *emocionado*. Dennis crouches by the bed to work on himself. *Que es lo que...*?
    Getting myself ready.
    Getting yourself what?
    I make it big, you know. Dennis's face is burning.
    Little shit!
    Now, now I'm ready, Dennis moans.
    Little shit!
    I'm coming! Better let me put it...
    Put it, *si, si sabe donde!*
    Shit!
    You little...
    Shit! cries Dennis, coming in his hand.
    Oh, hell! he moans. Oh hell. Why didn't you...
    Me. You comin' fore you in the door. *Que puedo yo*? Jesus, Maria, look at this, my spreadbed!
    Let me have another chance. It's you don't help me...
    Help you! You don't need no help! You *mancha* all my cubrecama, *asqueroso*! Help you! Jesus.
    You don't need no help!

Adie's messed her bed again. The birthday cake. Listen, Priscilla says to Megan after she's cleaned Adie up and put another load of sheets in the washer, I need a bath. Is it OK if I take one here?
Oh help yourself, says Megan.
So she goes upstairs and fills the huge old clawfoot tub on the third floor

and lowers herself gratefully into it.

Meanwhile, downstairs, the Astronomer advances over a sandy beach toward the camera and tosses back a forelock, smiling; Megan could just eat him up.

Earth's ancient dwellers studied the moon with instruments, believed they could see valleys, mountains there. They pondered, certainly, the possibility of travel, there, beyond, someday...

It's after nine and clouds are thickening. Dennis has gone home bawling, while Nelson Márquez, child of criminal tendency, has gone back to the hallways of the project, reclines on the stair of Building B to get a view of Janice Alvarado's panties. Up on the roof, Frostie's found the star called Arcrurus in Bootes.

Priscilla starts to doze against the sloping side of the old tub.

Young and Crippen are testing thrusters, putting on the suits they'll wear for re-entry. Just for practice this time. The cabin's chilly and the toilet doesn't function; but these are minor matters.

In the Second Century AD, the Astronomer continues on public television, a writer, Lucian of Samosata, wrote a book about a hero carried to the moon by waterspout. A Frenchman, Montgolfier, devised a taffeta container, filled it with hot air, and watched it rise.

Cold! cries Adie. They've let the fire go out! The little ones have nothing on but little summer shirts.

A Russian, Konstantine Tsiolkowsky, wrote a work about exploring space in which he advocated the use of multi-stage rockets, a mix of liquid hydrogen and oxygen was proposed as a means of achieving heights unheard of... But it was a physics teacher in Worcester, Massachusetts, who put the principle into practice by firing his first rocket on a cold March day in Auburn, Massachusetts.

Priscilla, who can hear the program through the old heat ducts of the house, catches herself slipping down into the water, sits up abruptly. I could drown if I'm not careful... She wonders if anyone ever croaked himself this way. Gandhi, thinks Priscilla at her leisure now. How could she not think of it? She must call Frostie. Gandhi perceived the central problem of our age. How to get what you need and yet not harm... It's all of our problem, she thinks. Gandhi, married off as a boy to a girl of his family's choosing...needed. Chose his need. Chose his need. She has chosen her need in moving back to Waltham. And previous to that she chose her want. Or rather she didn't choose. How careless she has been. She is appalled by herself. And now the debris of all these needs and wants lies around her. Well, she's cleaning it up. Like the river, she's working on it. Care for your own, care for the world. The only time she has to contemplate this is in the bath, and riding on her bicycle. But Gandhi lived with the same dilemma. You can live with the dilemma. That's what living is. One of the doctors at McLean's, a subtle Jew with the same name as a well known Israeli violinist, said to her:

You love all these people downwind of the reactor; do you love yourself? She remembers the expression on his face. The genuine curiosity. How careless she has been.

Father Bustamante takes the choir at the French Church through the Ave Verum. Eulalie is the only alto, unless you count Yvonne Aucoin who sings the melody an octave below the sopranos.

And meanwhile, upstairs in the kitchen of the First Congregational, Eula Toler and Gladys Schoolcraft in to set the tables for tomorrow's ladies' luncheon, watch the spoons jump, and lament the necessity to rent the chapel to these burgeoning latino cultists—galling that they outnumber their own congregation, sprinkled sparsely through the stately sanctuary, elderly and perishing, their young folks moved to Lexington and Belmont; only the Italian Catholics choose to build brick villas here in the Highlands as an expression of prosperity. Eula notes another soup spoon missing from the service, wonders if it made its way into the soup kitchen...

And meanwhile, also, Soledad, Priscilla's daughter, is sitting in Ramona's darkened parlor in the lap of a sailor friend of Felipe Márquez, Nelson's older brother. The sailor is fondling her buds through her jersey top.

Priscilla gets out of the tub and dries off. She uses the phone before she goes downstairs. Frostie answers.

It's Gandhi, she tells him.

Whoodi?

Gandhi. The greatest man our age.

Cold! cries Adie. They've let the fire go out. They didn't stoke it. Leave it all to me!

The sailor kisses Solie's neck. She's looking through his wallet, finds a picture of his mother a hospital card with blood type O. What's your type? he asks. She doesn't know. You ought to, you could bleed to death, he whispers in her ear. She shivers at this intimate remark. He's seventeen. Dropped out of school to join the Navy. She looks at his wrist. He's wearing an expensive watch. The black hairs on his arm curl over the gold band in a way she finds attractive. She turns to look in his good looking brown face, then looks away, overcome by shyness and nervousness. She doesn't know if her mother's home yet, if she's wondering where she is.

Most likely not. Her mother only cares about her union, about her brown lung workers. Before this, she only cared about her sit ins and her marches. She'll tell a lie, she'll say she had to go and help Nelson with his homework, and her mother will believe her. Nelson's schoolwork is the only thing that matters to her mother.

Cold! cries Adie. She's going to wet her diaper again. Cold! It comes. Delicious warmth. Her mother will come and change her before it turns cold.

Priscilla comes downstairs and sits with Megan till the program's over. In 1990, they'll be going off to Mars. Imagine it! says Megan. They're simulating settlements already. Just for practice. Already they're receiving applications. You have to be a vegetarian, non-smoker, have a sense of humor. Listen, nights, I hardly sleep. I think of interstellar travel. Yes! This putrefying orb, we will escape it. That's the meaning of all these disturbances. Six billion inhabitants we'll soon have. Think of it. You don't smoke, and you're a vegetarian.

Well, only off and on. I've lost my sense of humor too, Priscilla says.

Well, your son then, he'll go, cries Megan. Tell him not to smoke. Listen. We're the only animal that's not at home her on this Earth—that must wear clothing, spectacles, appliances of all sorts—that can't be comfortable in its fur. We're meant for something else, a journey, I just know it!

Maybe, says Priscilla, thinking about Solie. She forgot to ask Frostie was she home.

She'll tell her mother, Solie thinks, that she
was at her girlfriend's and got sick,

The sailor puts his finger in.
It hurts a little but feels nice too.

She can just lie there while he does it,
think of anything she wants.

Frostie never lies, she thinks.
Never lies and never cries; but she
was once the only…Daddy's little Solie.

Her grandmother Bemis bought her avocados
at the Banks Square Market, mashed them, fed her
from a china dish passed down from Auntie Rhee.

Then Frostie came and had the croup. Her daddy left;
her room was rented to a stranger, and
she had to sleep with Benno. That was when
they left off being like the families of other girls.

Have you given up that bicycle, Megan asks.
    No, I've bought a helmet though.
    Oh, wonderful. You'll be a quadro plegic, but at least your brain will be…Intact, ha ha! I wish that I could be around when we move out of here. You don't appreciate the opportunity you might have. I worry you won't

live long, though; you're too special. It's tedious people live the longest. Like that Fahey woman comes to clean…

If she tells me one more time about her husband's prostrate, and her granddaughter's photogenic memory… No Irish need apply. The wealthy used to post that in their windows.

It was this Fahey woman's type they had in mind. If she tells me one more time about her daughters I will cut my throat. I'm perfectly happy to have no progeny.

But you have a daughter.

Who did not chose to reproduce. A perfectly ordinary child she was. I don't know why I ever thought she might be special. She used to worry if she broke her fingernail. Music meant rock and roll to her.

Priscilla gets up to look in on Winnie. Sleeping with her mouth open. Dreadful to be seen in sleep.

Cold, cries Adie. Priscilla goes in to find her messed again. A sewer smell. Methane, she thinks. Someday they'll make a fuel from it. The washing machine is still filled with the earlier sheets. She moves them to the drier, rinses out the one she just took off. She's very tired suddenly. Two more hours till Rosa comes.

They've had to call in Rosa, thrown the whole schedule off. She pours detergent in again. So much detergent, so much water… They tried the plastic pads you throw away awhile, but they cost too much. She's heard that the Indians kept things sterile by in the sun: products of miscarriage, placentas, they used to hang in trees… Megan's asleep in front of the news. The Bruins have lost to Buffalo. A light fog likely after midnight. A carpenter from Hull has won a half a million in the lottery. He tells the Boston Globe reporter he'll report to work as usual tomorrow. Toshiko Seko is the favored runner in the Marathon this year. Food and heating oil prices up, while housing starts are… Priscilla wakes Megan, moves her into bed. Then sits to do her notes. Reads her earlier report: Clifford's bath, BM, Winnie's passage of three stools resembling blackberries, Adie's birthday party. Adds the brother's visit, loose bowels and Megan's going meekly off to bed following her favorite program…

She's brought her notes from the last Health Workers' Union Formation Committee to write up, but she barely gets started on them, when she puts her pen down to rest her eyes a moment and falls asleep.

Re entry

Eulalie brings 'How Amiable Are Thy Dwelling Places' home to practice, gives a couple dollars and a box of cream-filled donuts to Helen Schade Then, going into the bedroom, finds Alcide asleep on the floor, one hand clinging to his walker. La Schade probably never even looked in on him even once! She wakes him. I can't lift you. You have to get up yourself. He can't. Well, you'll have to lie there then till I can call the Agency in the morning. She hasn't the heart anymore to be angry. Gets his pillow and a blanket.

My Woman, he says, reaching for her.

I have the lump, she tells him. Tears come, finally, gratefully. She gets another pillow and stretches beside him and he reaches for her breasts. He knows them to be flaccid, hanging to her middle, but the skin is still white and smooth as when she was a girl, the nipples rather pale and maidenly in spite of suckling their one child till she was four. The thighs, too, silky, and the calves firm and muscular as he used to admire them winking under her ample skirts. He puts a nipple in his mouth and feels her loosen, open to him.

Megan wakes and rings the little bell. I slept an hour, she tells Priscilla. That was good. Maybe if I'm lucky I'll get another two. Priscilla standing by the window looks out on snow. In April, is it possible? No, it's only moonlight. I hear the ducks, says Megan. There, I think I'm finished. No, I'm not. Another moment. There, just let me look and see how much. It feels a good amount. Priscilla shows her. Yes, a good amount. It ought to let me sleep another hour...
     Cold, calls Adie.
     Or maybe not, says Megan.
     They've let the fire die. And Ma is dead and Pa is dead, and Adie is alone...cries Adie.
     First sensible remark she's made in months, says Megan.

Priscilla puts another blanket over Adie, and all is quiet.

It's after midnight and La Schade is settling in to watch The Movie Loft, a mystery with Peter Lore. Since the State she never goes to bed till three or later, as she pleases. She tries a donut, but her craving is for something salty, so she finds a jar of peanut butter, eats it off her finger. And Rosa wakes from her nap in front of the late news.

A Bemis bus has been hijacked they're reporting on channel 7. The passengers are taken safely home in a police van, and the driver is in custody…A Mr. Prasad…part time student at Boston University. His motive is unknown… A passenger with strawberry hair and two canes is being interviewed before she gets into a police van to be taken home. On the Late Show, Peter Lore, as Mr. Moto, builds a tower of matches on his table at the International Hotel.

Rosa throws cold water on her face, puts on her stockings and shoes and goes to the bus stop on Mount Auburn Street. The Fahey woman from down the street is already there with plastic bags of knitting, flip flops, large bottle of Pepsi—she makes herself comfortable--police radio she listens to all night. You going to sisters? I got Wolfie. Dirty bastard, she tells Rosa.

He's actually very kind and thoughtful when you get to know him, Rosa says, and sets her mouth against any further conversation, but Mrs Fahey doesn't notice. You can call me Rita, you know. We've known each other long enough.

I'd rather call you Mrs. Fahey, Rosa says. She thinks of Wolfie. Of their pleasures. She wonders if they know of it at the agency, if this Fahey woman knows it. His caresses drive her wild. Him too. Why should she deprive him? She recalls this morning. His hands on her belly, her breasts; his tongue up in her. Her womb leaping. Aah my darli, darli… Suppose that they know, now, that this Fahey woman's told. That she'll never again feel under his sleeping, slackened flesh to turn him in the bed at night. It will be this woman, interrupted in her knitting, or her eating, going to him without feeling, putting her hands on his sleeping flesh that is so alive in the mornings when she takes him in her kind and powerful hands to help him pee.

Did I show you the card my daughter sent me for my birthday? the Fahey woman asks. Must have cost five dollars if a cent. This big. It didn't fit in the mail slot. They had to leave it on the porch…

Yes, you showed me, it was very nice, says Rosa.

Always buy the best, my girls. My Vivie wants a blue Sedan de

Ville, but you have to wait five weeks you want a certain color, and she wants the black with red vinyl seats. And opera windows. So she'll wait, she says; she always was like that. Things have to be just so…

Priscilla takes Megan's bedpan and empties it.

She ought to sleep another hour if she can, thinks Megan. She sets out the Solar System in her mind's eye; sometimes that induces a couple hours of sleep, at least distraction: to let her mind range outward, like that unmanned Pioneer, our data scratched in its antenna; line drawings of a man, a woman, diagram of sun and planets. The Astronomer thinks it's highly likely that there's life on other planets. And not the green humanoids of science fiction, but something totally unexpected. He thinks it highly likely, too, that we'll pack up and move to other planets. Mars once had a better climate, might regain it…not just planets, either; the moons of Jupiter and Saturn are known to have an atmosphere like ours. And even asteroids… She wonders if the Universe is infinitely expanding, or contracting, hopes that it's the former. She doesn't like the thought of all this swirling like bath water down one of those what-you-call them, holes… She wishes she could understand this entropy. Will Bach and Beethoven be gobbled up, or will they, in the form of data, be flung out, that ultimate microsecond, to some other universe being born?

Rosa arrives, and wants to know where Margo is. They called me in, Priscilla tells her. She called the office, said she couldn't take it any longer. Megan says she thinks she's pregnant.

Ah, I just get home, they call me, Rosa says. I spend all the afternoon waiting for the Mayor to come for Adie's birthday.

She didn't enjoy it, and now she has the runs. I just finished changing her the fourth time. I have a second set of sheets in the washer now.

Dios! says Rosa. Well Megan enjoyed it a little bit. There was a woman played the harp. That woman with the two canes?

Yes, her name is Henrietta Rose.

I see her just now on the television! Rosa suddenly remembers the woman being interviewed
by channel 7.

You didn't!

Yes. A bus was hijacked. She was one of the people that they talked to.

A bus…

It is a man from India. The driver. He is all the way to Watertown when they stop him.

Why would a driver want to hijack a bus? It couldn't have been the driver.

Yes, they say it is the driver. Maybe he want to go back home. To his country.

India?

Supongo que sí.

It isn't possible to drive a bus to India, Rosa.

Oh, well, maybe he just can't stand it any longer. I get so I can just get on a bus and make them take me back to Xoyatla To Xoyatla you can drive a bus.

Ah, Rosa.

That Fahey woman's standing at the bus stop with me, going to Wolfie. She make me angry.

No Irish need apply.

What's that?

What Megan says about her. It's an old thing they used to say when the Irish first came over.

Now they say it about us.

Well, yes. I have to go. I left some notes. You can copy them and add your own. Just spell things the way I do. She puts her helmet on. She doesn't like to ride her bike this late. She had it snatched once, by some kid. A week later saw him, a big kid riding it past the CVS. She grabbed it, unthinking of the danger—a kid as big as she—and dumped him off. He came with a story about his father giving it to him; but she knew it was her Nishiki by the lamp Frostie had put on and by some rust spots she had scraped and painted with another blue not quite the same. You come down to the police and tell your story, she invited, and he ran off.

I never indulge in games of chance, says Mr. Moto's friend to an invitation to step upstairs. Mr. Moto accepts the invitation; and, under the pretext of composing a haiku, passes a note to his lady friend, instructing her to call police. The lady friend excuses herself to go to the Ladies, turns a corner and rushes to the phone booth, but it's occupied by a sailor talking French. Helen Shade, unable to bear suspense, tosses the cat off her lap and goes to the kitchen for more chips and surprises a cockroach in the sink. Priscilla coasts down Adams, then crosses a block to Moody where the lights are brighter. She'll get three hours sleep before she has to wake Solie for the early bus, and start rousing Benno who takes a full hour to really wake up. Someone is being tossed out of one of the bars on the corner of Chestnut. She hurries past and is flying past the corner of Norumbega Street when a light colored car, an old LTD or a Mercury, thinks an eye-witness, runs a stop and tosses her and her bicycle over the hood and drives on. And so it's happened, she thinks as she is flying upward, and almost as she'd imagined it... *Una caida aparatosa*, The expression passes through her mind just before losing consciousness. An apparatus-filled-fall. Bike and backback flying in different directions as she feels herself bounce off a hood and fall sideways to be deposited on the asphalt...The sailor is still talking interminably in French when Helen Schade returns to the movie with a plateful of chips and a bottle of green olives. And Priscilla comes to in a blur of faces, glasses gone. Don't move. Just lie there. Ran the stop. Light colored LTD. Or a Mercury. Ford product. This gentleman saw it. The eye-witness is a kid they call the Maggot. Out looking for a bottle he has stashed in one of the hedges along Norumbega. Helmet saved her. Lookit the crack in it, says the EMT. She moves her arms and legs a little. Nothing broken. But her glasses... No, don't move. But I'm... The ambulance is coming. But my bicycle. Cruiser'll take it in. But is it... Busted? Well the frame might be OK. The wheels are twisted. We'll take it in the station. You just lie there. And my glasses... Someone hands them to her, miraculously unbroken. Just relax. Your front wheel's a little bent, and the handlebars. It can be fixed. We'll keep it for you. You relax. She does. Three EMTs, efficient with scoop stretcher, wedge her in with sandbags. Collar on her neck. Relax and let them, she thinks, sorry for bad thoughts about police with Nelson earlier. Relax. She closes her eyes. Alive. Now she can think it. Now, her bicycle, her glasses all accounted for, she thinks about her life. Her life. The Fahey woman hears about the accident on police radio fifteen minutes after it happens. A nurses' aide on a bicycle. She calls Rosa at the Sisters. Mr Moto turns an ace up. It is said success in games, he tells his companion, is a sign of success in other... I would have sworn you had the Jack, says his companion. Megan tries reciting kings and queens of England. These galaxies over-excite her. She pauses first to savor Priscilla's visit. She hopes she's safely home. At least she's bought a helmet. Alive, Priscilla thinks.

How many times has she imagined this? Her broken body flung in the air, crushed under semi-trailers; never saw herself surviving. Helmet saved her. Lucky. How good life is. A beautiful young man is sitting at her feet. It's been a while since she could appreciate male beauty, she thinks. Another, darkly attractive, is fixing the pressure cuff. I think I'm perfectly all right, she says. Well, if you are, it's due the helmet, and the dark man shows her the crack inside the lining. The other shines a penlight in her eyes: follow finger... But I really think... The pupils are a bit... I really think if you'll just let me up... uneven, and the left a little slow. Or if you could leave me off at Varnum Circle. My kids... How many kids you got? Two, no, three... You sure? Yes, three, of course. I was forgetting younger. Before puberty, they were like puppies, children...you didn't worry...Street you live on? Why is he so severe with me? Spring Street, she says. Number eighty... no, that was before...Funny now I can't... Children's names? Well, Frostie, Sol...You just relax. A certain item, of interest to us both, has turned up in a curio shop in San Francisco, says Mr. Moto. Merchandise on which we both can profit. Megan starts with William the Conquerer who pretended to retreat, then fell on the flanks of Harold's English. William the Red, and his son, Rufus. Scoundrels... I believe that I'm perfectly all right, Priscilla says. This is a waste of taxpayer's money... She strains at the straps as the pull up the hill below the hospital. All the hospitals Pricilla's ever known have been on hills, she wonders why . Perhaps they're on the sites of the old TB sanatoriums, built there for the freshening winds, the coolness. Blue lights of Emergency. She's handed out and pushed through double doors and down the long passage where she came, how many hours ago? with her offering of blood for Terry. Bright lights. A curtain drawn around. What time is it? One-forty-five. Two nurses pull at her clothing: sweater, bluejeans...she's wearing, naturally, her oldest, yellowest brassiere. They struggle with it as the two young EMTs look on. You want to try, the nurses offer. You've more experience than us, this sort of thing. Priscilla laughs. Oh, life is good, she thinks. So let them, let them care for her. It's true she can't remember her address, had trouble remembering Benno's name... Benno's very existence! She recalls, now, carrying him to bed, his elbows and knees poking her, his finger to his cuspid. Henry the First, another scoundrel. White ship lost with heir and sister. Only the Butcher of Roen is saved to tell the tale. I'm perfectly awake, thinks Megan. Henry the Second: 'Is there no one here that can deliver me?' And four knights hear and cruelly stab his enemy Thomas, at the altar of St. Bennet. Rosa changes Adie, who's still oozing. She thinks of Wolfie's sleeping flesh, potent with manly emanations when she touches him, how the Fahey woman will be turning him as if he's some giant bothersome baby... They did it in the bedroom, once, she recalls; it wasn't successful, the bed requiring standard positions he wasn't able any more. Who has seen them? They always locked the door. She remembers the Fahey woman once saw her on the street when The Kisser caught her unaware and gave her a long buss. The look on her face. Probably right there she began to have dirty thoughts about Rosa. It's raining slightly, has turned warmer. The Professor, under the Gold Star Mothers' Bridge, sheds his coats, flings out an arm comfortably, discovers the Maggot isn't there beside him. Henry Second, thinks Megan, then Stephan, of whom nothing worse was known than that he was a usurper... The Maggot has felt an itch to have a shower and a woman, has engaged a room at the Maple Shade Hotel. Having witnessed an accident on the corner of Norumbega and Conant, he lopes toward Prospect. He hasn't found the woman he expected to pick up earlier at O'Reilly's Daughter, or even the other one that sometimes lurks outside the Indian bistro, he still has hopes, and has remembered the fifth of Wild Turkey hidden in the bushes outside the Irish Travel Bureau. The Professor, missing him, is having night thoughts: Old, he thinks. His bones are aching. Where did it go, his brutish youth? And now this senseless dotage. Why? So we may palpate, sing, and suffer Godhead out of every crack and crevice of Creation...? Admittedly, for some, the perspective is the Godhead's asshole, yes, but all, he swigs the last of the Lambrusco, all will be known. At the hospital, Priscilla's covered with a johnny and a blanket, wheeled to X-ray with her house key in one hand and her wallet on her stomach. These, she must have by her, so they've dug them for her out of her backpack. Gandhi, she remembers on the elevator. Did she tell Frostie? Yes, she called him. Benno was in bed and Solie not accounted for. Was she there? How could she not remember her baby? Must have been an awful bang. The greatest figure of our century was Gandhi, yes. And telling them she lived on Spring Street. What was she thinking? It was seven years ago, now, that she lived on Spring Street. Feeling rich after the divorce settlement, she did volunteer work and ran the PTA, lived in an apartment that cost three hundred a month, spent half the money on saving Frostie's dog's life after she was hit by a car. Months of bills at Angel Memorial Hospital. It was all they thought about for a whole year, that sweet beagle with the liquid eyes. And she was saved, but it always dragged, the leg. It took them just six months to go through the rest of the money, and end up sitting in the anterooms of welfare offices and charity clinics. Ross would have given more, of course. But she was proud and wouldn't take it. This was her idea and she must make it work, was her notion. And Ross must remarry. She would not ruin his life. And she wasn't ever worried. It was all a novelty. You act like you're on a Girl Scout camping trip, Ross told her when he visited the children once and found them all sleeping in sleeping bags on the floor of a two room apartment. He was full of scorn for her giddiness, but she'd have never got through it if she'd been properly serious….*Estrambótica*…A word Sr. Hugo used about her. *Por qué sois tan estrambótica?* Three pictures are taken of her head. It isn't cracked, they tell her after a fifteen minute wait. Richard the Lion Hearted, kicked the Duke of Austria. Crusader Richard, he whose enemy, Saladin, on hearing he was ill, sent fruit fresh from Damascus, snow from mountaintops. The doctor will be with her shortly, they tell Priscilla. My glasses? The nurse steps forward, hands her the pair of aviator glasses that she got from the poor box back in the days when she was orchestrating public welfare. At the sisters, Rosa dozes. She loves these quiet, small hours when her body goes slack yet not quite into sleep. Funny how you have to be at least a little awake to appreciate sleep. It's always bothered her to miss deliciousness of sleep because it's a time stolen from you by oblivion. Helen Schade has dozed and waked again to the flickering black and white…'Can I be certain,' says Mr. Moto's companion, 'you are what you seem?' 'We are, both,' says Mr. Moto, 'in the same business, one might say…' And in the meantime, young Mr. Hitchings and the nightclub singer have been trussed up in a vault because they 'know too much.' Helen's missed that part, but has seen it all before. The voices have started up again. And someone has tapped her shoulder as she slept. And stolen her breath. She can only get a scant amount of air into her lungs. It feels like a need to yawn that's been prevented. The black and white cat lies like a lion couchant on her breast and breathes into her face. She rises, upsetting him toward the floor and his claws scrabble into her ribs. A shot! They've killed Mr. Moto. No. He's wearing his steel weskit, rises from the floor, and at that moment, the police, at last… The doctor, Dr. Yee—she reads his nametag—stands over Priscilla. You have a slight concussion he tells her, exquisitely, orientally polite. You will stay here, and be observed until tomorrow. There is nothing, really, to be worried... Have you pain? No pain. And can you touch your chin to your chest? She can. She looks around the shiny cubicle...a gift of Dr. and Mrs. Morton Bloomberg, says the plaque on the door. Oh, good, yes, life is...all these people caring for her, telling her, relax, and let us...And she, one of the Players in the Great Orchestra of Life, a term her father used to quote from some old book. *Estrambótica.* Means eccentric. Yes, she is eccentric in the tradition of the Rowans. What of Madsens, she wonders. She thinks it must be Madsens in her that make her want to make an honest workman of Nelson. Rika had left The Watch behind her, but Priscilla knew her grandfather, Oscar Madsen, till she was ten. He spent his retirement in the basement of the house on Myrtle Street, in his workshop. Making something useful out of things he found in the neighbors' trash. And Grandmother Hulda in the kitchen. Cooking. Joyful cooking. Where had that got lost? The second movie starts, but Helen Schade wanders down the hall in darkness, fleeing voices...Megan, still wide awake, ticks off Henry Fourth. High-spirited Hal, the Fifth. His marchers mowed down the French at Agincourt. Red Roses here, and white. She never can keep them straight... Fleeing voices, Helen, runs out her door and down the steps in mules and housecoat, over dewy grass to sidewalk, stubbing her toe on a sprinkler head, turning into Moody street and into the arms of Maggot. Jesus! Jesus! Women have been slipping through Maggot's fingers the entire... Edward of York. Another usurper. Queen Margaret wandering about the countryside with Henry's sons...The Fahey woman calls the sisters'. Rosa, startled, answers. That girl that rides a bicycle. On police radio...What girl? The one that rides a bicycle. Comes to the sisters...Who is this? It's Rita. Are you asleep or something? Oh, Mrs. Fahey...Did you hear what I said? ...hit by a car. Yes, that girl that rides a bicycle. A hit and run. They haven't found the car.

White Mercury, they're saying...Priscilla! Yes, that was her name. Hit! She just leave here. Two hours ago... Thrown over the hood, the Fahey woman says with satisfaction. And didn't stop. A Ford make of car, they're saying. She was there, you say...Yes, they call her in for Margo. Oh, Margo, yes. She's preggers, did you know? No. How do you know? I just know. Just how you know the things I do with Wolfie, Rosa thinks. Bad magic. She wants to hang right up. But Priscilla! Is she OK? Who? Priscilla! Rosa screams. Oh, I suppose. They took her to the hospital. I guess you like her. Yes, I like her. Cold fish, I'd say. She never gives me time of day. And whoever heard of riding a bicycle... I keep her, Rosa thinks. I ought to let her go. She has her helmet on, and I keep talking... Girl with a college education, says the Fahey woman. What is she doing riding around changing diapers? Myself, I only do these couple nights to keep me busy. Mr. Fahey gives me anything I want. He asks me the other day, do I want to go to one of these islands down there where they have pools with bars floating in them like little islands; you swim up and get your drink... They say she is alive? Rosa shouts. I told you they took her to the hospital. That's all they say. And you needn't shout. I've never had a problem with my hearing! says the Fahey woman with dignity. But Rosa has hung up.

...the space ship Columbia's been turned, is traveling tail first now, and right side up.

Tide turns, Henry's brought from the tower, crowned, then killed. That villain, Uncle Richard—he has one shoulder higher than the other—puts the two young princes in the tower... Keeping me awake, these kings and martyrs, Megan thinks. Refractory! calls Winnie out of sleep. Recalcitrant! Antonia wakes with a pain in her side and opens the Bible beside her bed: *And also in the night my heart instructs.* Maggot passes Helen Schade the paper sack with Wild Turkey as he guides her over Ash Street to the room he's rented at the Maple Shade Hotel. She, though not a drinker, downs it. Whoa there! Save a mite. They finish it in the room, and fall into the bed without a further introduction... Tudors next. Megan loves the Tudors. Katherine of Aragon, that's Isabella's daughter. Isabella rode in chain mail into battle with her troops. Anne, then, Jane. Heads roll. Sir Thomas More, the wife of Pole. She ran around the scaffold: 'If you want this head, you'll have to catch me!'

The astronauts are given final go. The orbit rocket fires.

The Maggot doesn't like the smell of this woman, decides to take her in the shower and wash both their bodies with a bar of Palmolive soap provided by the hotel. And then their hair, with some Herbal Essence Shampoo left behind by a previous guest. Her body isn't bad, although she seems to be missing a breast. And her hair is long and golden. Helen looks where her right breast used to be and sees the evil face of a surgeon, plotting with her sister… She must get a lawyer. Are you a lawyer by any chance? she asks the Maggot. No, but I know lots of them, he tells her. In the morning I'll take you to them. He gives her another drink from the bottle and takes her back to bed. A nurse comes in to take Priscilla's vital signs. They are all normal. They've called the house for her and all her children are accounted for. You know I couldn't remember how many I had. Well it was quite a bump, I guess. Yes, they showed me the helmet. It's all cracked. A woman named Rosa called to ask if you were alive. We told her you were. She was so upset. She thought she killed you, keeping you late to tell you about that bus that was hijacked…It couldn't have been hijacked, Priscilla says. A bus driver wouldn't hijack his own bus. They can't have been thinking straight… The Fahey woman is burning toast in Wolfie's kitchen. Megan wonders whether Isabella rode side saddle into battle, or astride. With armor, she must have ridden astride. Her daughter can't have been as formidable a character to be discarded so easily; and she is followed by a flock of equally weak sisters: Anne of Cleves, Great Flanders Mare; more Katherines: Parr and Howard. A son reigns briefly, Edward; gloomy Catholic Mary. Glorious Elizabeth. She knew how to handle men. Elizabeth would have ridden astride had it been called for. Now Stuarts. Scottish cousin James. His Sowship. Baby Charles First, brought over a crowd of unpleasant priests and lost his head. She's getting drowsy now, of course, when it's too late. For the sun is striking the windows of the Nichols wing of the hospital. The nurse shines a light in Priscilla's eyes. You're fine. The doctor will be in at seven. She will go home. Will she go to work? Who will relieve Rosa? She ought to go to sleep an hour at least, but her thoughts won't allow… *Una felicidad rara.* She must preserve it. Preserve. Like her grandfather in his basement workshop. Preserve, remake, make useful again. Herself. Herself first. Yes. How can Solie care about her life when it was she who saw her mother… You will stay home from work I'll assume, the nurse says. OK, she says, relieved. She's sure Rosa will stay if necessary. Solie, yes, who saw her mother take that knife…She must sleep. She feels beckoned into sleep.

Sun now strikes the bars of Billy's cage;
he ruffles feathers, ticks and chuckles.
Obfuscation! Winnie crows…
strikes under a broken blind at the Maple Shade Hotel,

and into Maggot's…Mandible, says Winnie.

There'll be no sleeping now, thinks Megan,

and she picks up a copy of Opera News and switches on the light. One of the earliest lessons that Nell Rankin mastered was to sing the CEGC arpeggio in a single breath.

At an altitude of one hundred and seventy miles over the Indian Ocean, two maneuvering rockets fire on the command of a computer…

She, Nell Rankin, could hold the notes for eight beats each, ascending and descending. Maggot studies the lock of last night's platinum upon the pillow: Jesus! Get your clothes on! Jesus. How old are you? You must be sixty. Jesus. You liked me well enough an hour ago. No beauty, kid, yourself, says Helen Schade. In a dream, Eulalie Arsenault is present at the interment of a leg—her own. Its multiple perfections are the subject of discussion among the Robichauds and Aucoins present. But suddenly it turns into a monstrous purple horror. The Maggot takes another drink and falls back to sleep. Helen Schade, thinking of her cat, gets up and dresses. The alcohol has shifted her thoughts a bit. She wonders has she left the door open? Her little room with hotplate, share a bath! She must get back…Get out, the Maggot mutters. Go the back stair.

And don't let no one see you!

Earth's Gravity

*..retrorockets finish firing, slow the spaceship just enough to drop out
of orbit into the pull of Earth's gravity*

Looking down in her dream, Eulalie notes
she's standing not on her remaining leg,
but a couple of inches above the ground and rising...
And when Rosa comes in to get up Megan to
the toilet, she shows Rosa a color photo
of Fernando Corena in a production of
Elisir d'Amore, descending to
the stage of the old Metropolitan in a
splendid hot air balloon.

———————————————

$\mathbf{B}$arbara de la Cuesta has one published novel, *The Spanish Teacher*, winner of the Gival Press Novel Award in 2007. She has published stories in *The Texas Quarterly, The New Orleans Review*, and *The New American Review*, and received Fellowships from the Ragdale Foundation, The Virginia Center, and The Millay Colony where she completed *Rosamundo*.

Though she now lives in New Jersey where she still teaches languages, for many years she lived and taught English as a Second Language in the city of Waltham, Massachusetts. There she was fortunate to have an opportunity, to come to know some extraordinary students among the latest waves of immigrants. As well, through her work in an elder facility, she became acquainted with older immigrants retired from the historic woolen mill and the watch factory. A fellowship from the Massachusetts Artists Foundation enabled her cobble together a living from these part-time jobs and have time to take notes on her surroundings and begin *Rosamundo*.

www.ingramcontent.com/pod-product-compliance
Lightning Source LLC
Chambersburg PA
CBHW021149090426
42740CB00008B/1014